"SHE WASN'T BORING." ♡ ZELDA FITZGERALD

FASHION'S WHO'S WHO SHOW YOU HOW TO

MAKE LIFE BEAUTIFUL

FASHION'S WHO'S WHO SHOW YOU HOW TO

MAKE LIFE BEAUTIFUL

CAMILLA MORTON

HUTCHINSON

1 3 5 7 9 10 8 6 4 2

Hutchinson
20 Vauxhall Bridge Road
London SW1V 2SA

Hutchinson is part of the Penguin Random House group of companies whose
addresses can be found at global.penguinrandomhouse.com.

Copyright © Camilla Morton 2015
Text design © carrdesignstudio.com
Photos copyright see page 240

Camilla Morton has asserted her right to be identified as the author of this
Work in accordance with the Copyright, Designs and Patents Act 1988.

First published by Hutchinson in 2015

www.randomhouse.co.uk

A CIP catalogue record for this book is available from the British Library.

ISBN 9780091959081

Printed and bound by C&C Offset Printing Co. Ltd
Designed by carrdesignstudio.com

This is dedicated to

Fashion's greatest Fairy Godmother, Joan Burstein,

Michael Howells, for always being right,

Alexander Fury for breaking my ankle…

CONTENTS

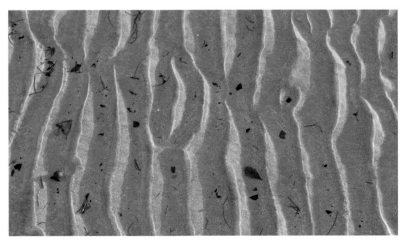

"I am inspired by women and I design to inspire women. So when I think about beauty, I think about women. Character. Intelligence. Strength. Style. That is beauty – perfect in its imperfections. The first woman who ever inspired me was my mother, Lily. She had all of that. She taught me very early on that fear is not an option. This lesson empowered me to take risks, to go for it, and it has made me the woman I am today.

Even when I was young, I was never interested in being a little girl; I always wanted to be a woman. I dreamed of being glamorous and free. I didn't always know what I wanted to do, but I was clear about the kind of woman I wanted to be. I longed to be independent, to travel the world, to have a career of my own. Now that I have become that woman, I like to inspire other women to do the same – to find the beauty within and achieve confidence and self-reliance. The most important relationship is the one you have with yourself.

As a child growing up in Brussels, I nurtured this relationship, spending many hours alone, reading and planning and daydreaming. I found beauty in the forests surrounding the city. I would walk and walk, making plans, imagining the places I would go, the woman I would become. Even now, I love to hike for inspiration and to find clarity.

Nature is my source of strength and an endless source of beauty. For me, clarity is a very important part of creativity. If I have clarity, I can make things happen, and I love to make things happen. It is one of the greatest gifts of being a designer. I love to capture the way the light falls through the trees and turn it into a print, or to have the soft whisper of a Mediterranean breeze become a chiffon skirt on the latest wrap dress. For me, inspiration is about paying attention. Whether travelling or curled up in my studio with my iPad, I have always been curious. If you are curious, there is beauty to be found everywhere.

So go for it and enjoy it all!

Diane von Furstenberg

"My dad made me a Wendy house when I was four. It was white with a glossy bright red front door and pink roses painted round the door-frame. My mum made little curtains for the windows and bedding to go with the mini bunk-beds they'd made for my teddy bears. It wasn't plywood and paint to me – it was perfect. I was lucky – I grew up with bedtime stories read to me, where all the characters had different voices, that took me to a different faraway land every night. I knew that castles could be made out of washing-up liquid bottles and cardboard boxes and that treasure came from the riches of your imagination. Who says everything has to change when you grow up?

Just because you don't dress up as a fairy every day doesn't mean you should forget that sparkle.

One of the things I love most about fashion is that same sense of awe that the beauty and invention of the shows evoke. From the very first time I snuck backstage I was hooked. Here was a wonderland where *anything* goes; where the clothes told stories and could transform you into a dazzling fairy princess, a warrior, or whoever you wanted to be, with options for all occasions gliding up the runway. Here Cinderellas wore Manolo Blahnik heels that didn't get lost at midnight. It seemed the nearest point to heaven – a creative Camelot where ideas were formed, and it was fun, not work. For me, the magic of fashion is those moments of creative brilliance – it's being pulled into the whirlwind of these creative minds; it's exquisite high tea at Claridges with my Fashion Fairy Godmother Mrs. B., or it's running round the galleries and feeling inspired with one of my designer friends. What really makes life beautiful is the people you share it with. That's why I asked some of the people that matter to me most to help me compile with love this ultimate fashion Who's Who of How To for you.

I don't claim to be the best cook, the best designer or the best crafter, but luckily I have best friends who are. Turn off the internet, turn on your imagination and let a host of the most creative names in fashion show you how to make the everyday even more beautiful. Indulge in some creative frivolity – you don't have to, but why not? Let coat hangers take you to Ascot, give scarecrows some style or make biscuits that become jewelled buckles. From a high tea made of felt, or lips that are good enough to eat, the most important label is that of your own imagination. From paper windmills to a runway of designer paper dolls and a theatre to stage all your (mini) dramas, this is a book of ideas where a cup of tea is a work of art and beauty is in the eye of the beholder. A sense of adventure and having fun – that's what makes life beautiful. "

CAMILLA MORTON

PAPER DOLLS

Fashion should focus on fun and being fabulous. Look good. Feel good. Hot from the international runways are exclusive looks created in New York by Diane von Furstenberg and Thakoon; in London by Roksanda; and in Paris by Jean Paul Gaultier. Take your template and dress her up. From model casting to runway glory, from book marking to high tea or a trip to the opera, it's time to dress up, strike a pose, and let these paper dolls take your imagination on a fashionable adventure.

DIANE VON FURSTENBERG

THAKOON

ROKSANDA

JEAN PAUL GAULTIER

PRÊT-À-PORTEA

"About ten years ago we came up with the idea of reinterpreting the current catwalk and fashioning it into cake. So it is with great pleasure that I've taken a paper doll and turned her into Diane von Furstenberg."
MOURAD KHIAT

PRÊT-À-PORTEA
DESIGNER GINGERBREAD LADIES

YOU WILL NEED:

200g unsalted butter

35g icing sugar

127g flour, plus extra
for dusting

2g ground ginger –
approx. ¼ tsp

10g egg white – approx.
½ white from 1 small
egg

Rolling pin

Knife

Greaseproof paper

Baking tray

Icing sugar, water and
food colouring for
decoration, as required

Makes ten

THE MAKE:

1. Create a template of the paper doll in underwear (see p. 4) (you'll be layering up her look post bake) by tracing the silhouette onto baking paper.

2. Mix together butter, icing sugar, flour and the ground ginger until it reaches a crumble-like consistency.

3. Add the egg white then mix together until it forms a dough.

4. Let this rest in the fridge for at least 2 hours.

5. Now to fashion up your designers. Lightly dust a clean work surface with flour and roll out the dough until it is an even ½ cm in thickness – don't roll it too thin or you'll be liable to break limbs. Place in the freezer for 20 minutes before you cut your shapes. Pre-heat the oven to 180°C/gas mark 4.

6. Cut around your template using a sharp knife.

7. Carefully place your ladies on a baking tray, lined with greaseproof paper, and bake in pre-heated oven for 8 minutes. Do not let them tan too much.

8. Remove and allow to cool on a wire rack while you line up your icing and accessories and get ready to style.

9. Fashion her up with icing, using the paper doll instructions as inspiration. Mix your icing colours then outline and fill spaces as desired. Start with big shapes – dress, body – and end with smaller details such as sunglasses.

10. Leave the icing to set overnight at room temperature and your lady will be ready to lunch – or, more likely, to be served with tea.

NICHOLAS KIRKWOOD

"I have always liked folding and twisting paper to create little shoes. I used to do this when I was growing up – they must have been the first shoes I made.

Sometimes it's the simplest things that are the most effective. You could use these origami boots as decorations, ornaments, or turn them into jewellery – it's up to you. It feels good to step away from your desk, work or computer, and do something a bit creative, so fold some paper and create a moment of calm. These boots are really graphic and loads of fun!"

NICHOLAS KIRKWOOD ORIGAMI BOOT

YOU WILL NEED:

Square piece of paper (see template on p. 221) – paper napkins work brilliantly too

THE MAKE:

1. Fold paper in half lengthways, print facing out.

2. Fold in half lengthways again.

3. Make centre line crease to act as a guide then fold one half over at right angle.

4. Repeat and fold next corner in to create a point.

5. Fold triangle on the right in on itself.

6. Repeat on the other side.

7. Fold triangle in half on itself.

8. Rotate so that right angle is in the same direction as the image.

9. Fold up 'tail' of top triangle to create right angle with 'toe' of boot.

10. Fold down excess triangle on under wing then bend this whole wing round and tuck lower corner into toe triangle.

11. Puff and shape to open the boot.

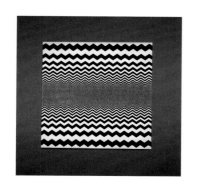

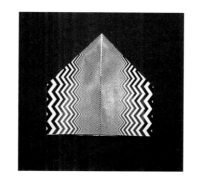

MATTHEW WILLIAMSON

Nature is at the heart of my designs and the more exotic the inspiration the better: far-flung countries and sun-drenched landscapes are really what capture my imagination. But similarly, back home, nothing beats a walk on Hampstead Heath with my dogs, Mr Plum and Coco. I love the silence, sunlight and space. When I'm travelling, I find inspiration in the unexpected unique finds in markets or surprising colour combinations in architecture rather than the typical sunset or white sandy beach. I am forever on the lookout. This year I went to the Maldives and Bali – I always return to my studio, and weave the things I saw back into my work; hibiscus flowers, bright basket weaves and swallowtail butterflies . . .

I grew up in Manchester but even when I was young, I was conscious of how grey it was. I always knew I wanted to be a designer. My mum was the biggest influence on me – she was a woman who knew how to dress and knew the power of style. My parents used to give me free rein in my bedroom to let loose creatively. I was so proud of it and was always changing it – the very last time I decorated it I chose a ghastly lavender shade from Homebase with silver paint for the woodwork . . . I even made the curtains! I still love creating interiors; making a space that reflects who you are is one of the most rewarding experiences possible.

The first fashion outfits I made were for my girlfriends when I was a teenager. There was definitely a gold ra-ra skirt! A dress for my Central Saint Martin's graduation collection was made from scraps of lace I swept up from Zandra Rhodes' floor, where I was interning at the time.

This project taps into the DNA of my brand. It's all about the exotic escape and wearing something with a free-spirited attitude; it's the combination of cool and warm colours – a deep red and cool turquoise, like Kate Moss in my first collection, Electric Angels.

Fashion has such a transformative quality. The daily ritual of getting ready is about comfort as well as projecting our personalities. My aim in life is to make women look and feel beautiful. This is what drives me and makes me happy.

Make a
MATTHEW WILLIAMSON SUMMER SILK SCARF DRESS

YOU WILL NEED:

2 large scarves or sarongs
(not necessarily matching print)

Needle

Thread

Scissors

Measuring tape or ruler

Ribbon, for neckline, at least 60cm

Silk cord, at least 160cm, or a belt, ribbon or necklace to accentuate waist

THE MAKE:

1. To create the neckline, take a scarf and fold down one of the four corners. This will be the top of your dress so decide which direction you prefer your pattern.

2. Stitch this fold in place, being sure to leave a gap (approx. 5cm) wide enough for your ribbon to run through.

3. Repeat these steps on your second scarf, so you have a back and front to your dress.

4. Lay the two scarves on top of each other so that the folds and shapes align. Starting roughly 33cm from the top (enough space for your arms), stitch the front and back together and continue until your skirt has finished and the split has begun.

   NOTE: The more you stitch up the less skin you will show.

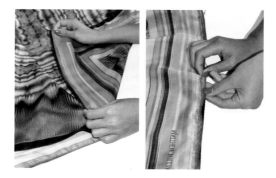

5. Slip the ribbon through the holes you have created at the neckline and link into the second scarf.

6. To create a belt, plait (just like you would your hair) at least 160cm of silk cord and use it to pull in your dress at the waist.

PAUL SMITH

I started cycling when I was eleven years old, and started racing when I was twelve. I spent a lot of my childhood dreaming of becoming a professional, which sadly never happened. I'd cycle all over the place. I'd ride to races, do the race and then ride all the way home. I spent a lot of time on the roads in Derbyshire, near my hometown of Nottingham. It's a really beautiful place with just huge open spaces.

When I was cycling it was taken pretty seriously and the idea of customising your bike didn't really occur to people. Today urban bike riding is more playful, full of energy and enjoyment, and I thought this project was a way of reflecting that.

As they say, 'beauty is in the eye of the beholder', so whatever you may consider to be beautiful, even something less obvious, can be beautiful. England is an incredible place in terms of its landscape and its geography but also in the minds of the people that live here. People are very open and quite lateral in the way they think about things. There's an enormous number of places in England that are beautiful, far too many to mention: Yorkshire, Derbyshire, Cornwall and many, many more. Get out on a bike and discover what's beautiful rather than getting stressed out; work hard at avoiding inheriting the troubles of the world.

Make a

PAUL SMITH
CUSTOMISED BICYCLE

YOU WILL NEED:

Scissors

Decorative, thick and electrical tape

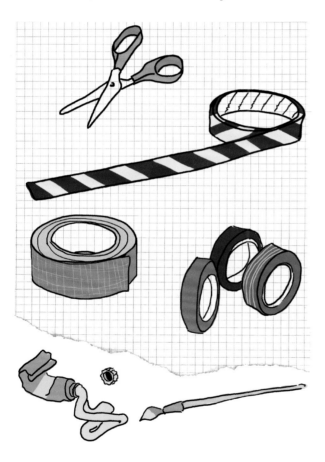

Tip

Try customising your own tape by painting masking tape with your own choice of acrylic paint.

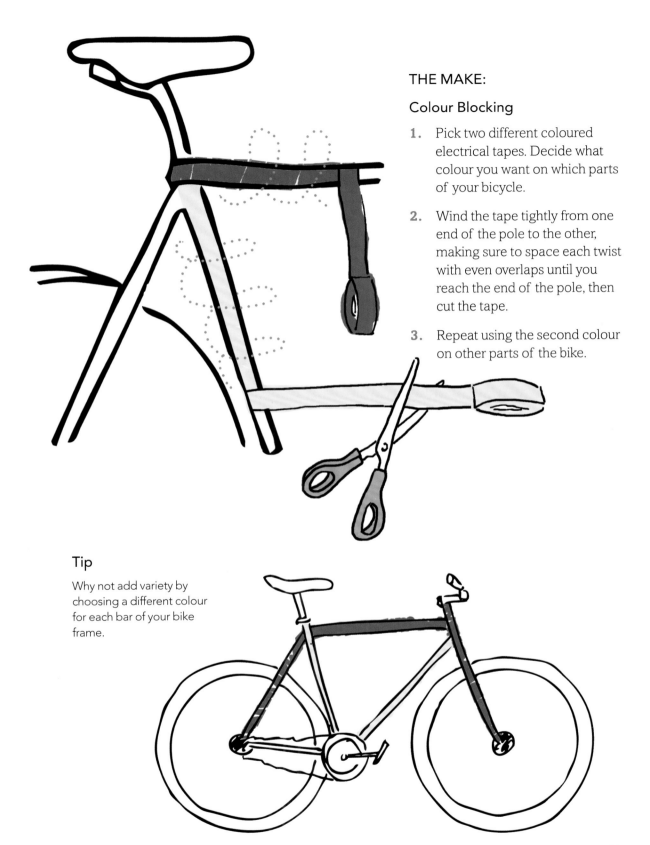

THE MAKE:

Colour Blocking

1. Pick two different coloured electrical tapes. Decide what colour you want on which parts of your bicycle.

2. Wind the tape tightly from one end of the pole to the other, making sure to space each twist with even overlaps until you reach the end of the pole, then cut the tape.

3. Repeat using the second colour on other parts of the bike.

Tip

Why not add variety by choosing a different colour for each bar of your bike frame.

Get Stripy

1. Choose different tapes and colours that will combine to make a nice stripe design (the possibilities are endless). Electrical and heavy duty adhesive tapes are best for withstanding all the elements.

2. One colour at a time, tightly wrap the tape around different sections of the bicycle.

Tip

Emphasise colour versus stripes by adding stripes to just one bar or the handlebars instead of covering the entire frame.

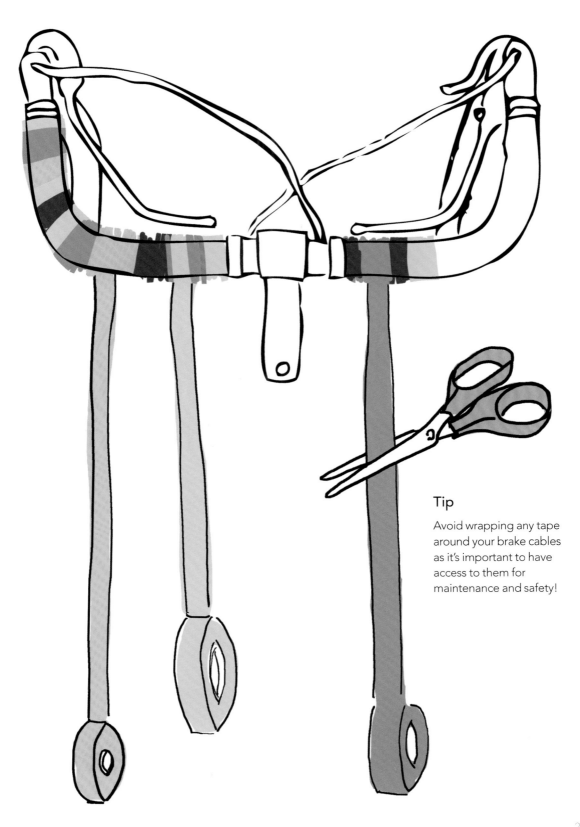

Tip

Avoid wrapping any tape around your brake cables as it's important to have access to them for maintenance and safety!

FABERGÉ

"Between 1885 and 1917 Peter Carl Fabergé created spectacular Easter eggs for the Russian Imperial family. Fabergé considered himself 'an artist-jeweller'. Each of his eggs took a specific theme and was layered with cultural references that celebrated life through memories crafted from vivid enamels and gemstones.

Flowers are a recurring motif in Fabergé's work and their joyful colours and form remain an inspiration for the house of Fabergé today. Now it is your turn: make life beautiful by creating a unique and ephemeral Fabergé-inspired egg made of flowers."

Make a
FABERGÉ EGG

YOU WILL NEED:

Oasis block (florists' foam)

Knife and spoon

Paint and paint brush

Cloves

Binding wire

Cocktail sticks

Kalanchoe (or small, fresh seasonal flowers)

THE MAKE:

1. Carve an egg shape out of the foam with a kitchen knife, then use your hands to mould the oasis until you have a smooth, symmetrical shape.

2. To make the egg stand upright, flatten the bottom or create a stand. If you are going to hang it, now is the time to push a piece of wire with a bend, or 'knot', at the bottom, through the egg and gently bend the other end of the wire to create a hook at the top.

3. Alternatively you could make a 'surprise egg', which opens out to show the inside as well as the shell. To do this, cut the egg shape in half, then hollow out the middle with a spoon, leaving a square base for the egg to stand on.

4. Leave the foam to soak in a bowl of water overnight until all the water has been absorbed.

5. Now you can start to decorate. Make a small hole with a cocktail stick and gently push the flowers (seasonal or wild with stems around 1cm long) into the hole. You may also like to punctuate your design with scented cloves, which can be painted in different colours. One by one, start to cover the egg. If you're making a 'surprise egg', start inside and then work your way out. Keep the foam on a moist plate and store in the fridge or leave in a cool place until you have covered the whole egg.

6. Display your creation – an egg like no other.

BELLA FREUD

"The spirit of anarchy and rebellion has always inspired me. My heart soars at the sight of any revolutionary artwork or the sight of a demonstration. It is exhilarating when people get together to resist and protest against complacency.

For this project I was thinking of how someone might want to make a jumper of their own, and give it some toughness to show they really mean it. The little gold safety pins are quite beautiful and recognisable. Writing a word in pins immediately gives it some double meaning. Something gentle like LOVE written in pins has the undercurrent of the anguish that can go with the love… And for anyone not interested in the dark side, they are nice and gold and shiny. I don't call the words slogans as a slogan is a mantra, telling people what to think or feel. I try to avoid that at all costs.

I find reading is the best way to allow my mind to leap into something new and that is what makes life beautiful – feeling a surge of interest in a new idea. How you make life beautiful is up to you. I find if I am organised I feel really free and that makes me happy. Chaos is the enemy of creativity. Just ordinary stuff like walking in the park with my dog, being with the people I love and thinking of how to do something new: that's what makes me feel alive. "

Make a

BELLA FREUD
PUNKED JUMPER

YOU WILL NEED:

Safety pins

Plain jumper

THE MAKE:

1. Lay your jumper flat and decide what you want to say.

2. Put the safety pins in position.

3. Rather than piercing the wool, secure the pins to your jumper with a small stitch in the eye and at the base.

WILD AT HEART

"After a brief stint in advertising, I was involved in arranging the flowers for a close friend's wedding and absolutely loved it. So I got an apprenticeship with a florist and worked my way up from there.

I have a wonderfully creative, dedicated team who work with me. A lot of our inspiration comes from the flowers and their personalities. My favourites are roses: gorgeously scented, so luxurious and classic, they're beautiful throughout their lifespan.

I feel so lucky that the nature of my job means I'm surrounded by beautiful colours, textures, scents and shapes all day and that we can use that beauty to enhance the most breathtaking events and romantic weddings. Here I'm showing you how to fashion an old-school corsage from an orchid – why leave something that beautiful at home?" NIKKI TIBBLES

Make a

WILD AT HEART
FRESH FLOWER CORSAGE

YOU WILL NEED:

Wire (thin and thick gauge)

Green gutter tape or florists' parafilm tape

Double satin ribbon, in a colour which complements your corsage

2 bombastic spray roses

1 phalaenopsis orchid flower

2 single ivy leaves

THE MAKE:

1. With a delicate touch and a steady hand, carefully 'wire' the flowers and ivy leaves by lining the stems with the thin-gauge wire.

2. Gently wrap the wires with gutter tape so the wire is concealed, as well as secured to its flower.

3. Tie the flowers and ivy leaves to the centre of a piece of thick-gauge wire that is long enough to wrap around your wrist so that it is neither too tight nor too loose.

4. Cover the wire in gutter tape and cut to the correct length for your wrist.

5. Gently thread the ribbon through the wire at the back of the flowers.

6. Twist the ribbon round the wire on either side of the flowers and tie in a knot at the end of the wire, leaving enough ribbon to be used to tie the corsage to the wrist.

7. Bend the wire around the wrist and tie the ribbon using a bow. Now all you need is a dashing date before waltzing off into the night.

 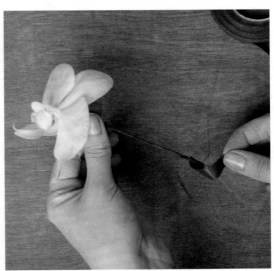

HENRY HOLLAND

> Believe in who you are. Positivity and self-belief make great things happen. Making life beautiful is another way of attracting beautiful things to your life, whatever mask or face you wear. And for me, life is about wearing glasses. Everything is more beautiful when it's in focus!

Make a

HENRY HOLLAND
DISGUISE

YOU WILL NEED:

Card

Copy of the template or
your own design

Elastic

Scissors

Pout

CUT

THE MAKE:

1. Carefully cut out Henry and stick onto card. If only it were always this easy to be someone else for a day.

2. Cut out the holes for the eyes and enough room for your nose. You're going to run into problems if you wear glasses.

3. Pierce holes and attach elastic or ribbon either side by the ears.

4. Head off to a party and see if your new guise is on the guest list; only don't leave them your tab…play nicely.

BRITISH FASHION COUNCIL

" London is known as one of fashion's most creative capitals. In February and September London Fashion Week hosts press and buyers from around the world that come to see the latest ideas at shows, events and presentations all over the city.

Each and every designer has their own point of view, and this should be celebrated as it's their creativity that makes London stand out. Each season we at The British Fashion Council work with a different designer to create an exclusive tote bag. Now you can create your own Fashion Week tote bag statement using these brilliant designs as inspiration. London has always been champion of the new, the unexpected and the innovative – be adventurous in your creation, and who knows where tomorrow will take you. "

Make a
BRITISH FASHION COUNCIL
TOTE BAG

YOU WILL NEED:

Plain tote bag

Tracing paper

Pencil

Fabric paints or marker pens

THE MAKE:

1. Photocopy and enlarge our illustration and pick the elements you'd like to use to embellish your plain tote bag.

2. You need a pass, notebook, sunglasses, lipstick – one or two? – phone, invites . . . You make the edit and build up your design.

3. Once you've traced the elements onto the bag, colour with fabric pens.

4. Leave to dry while you focus on your Fashion Week outfit.

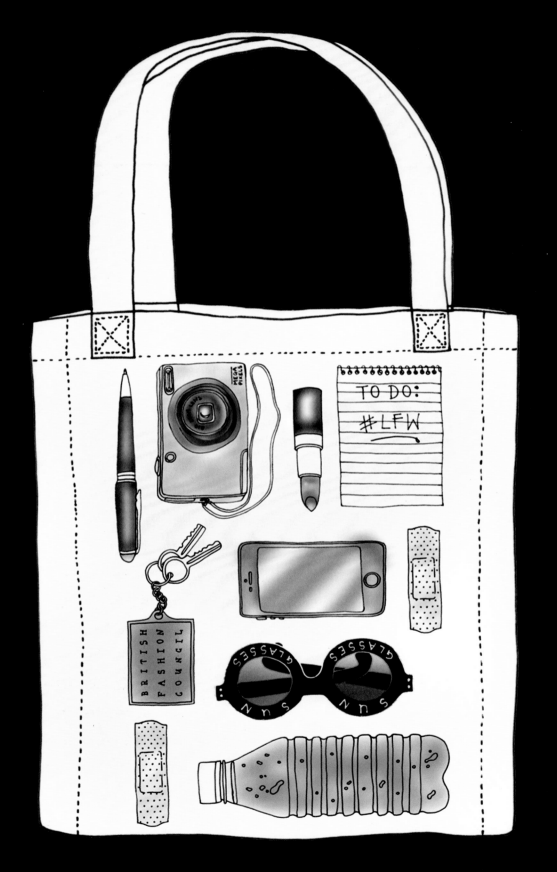

STEPHEN JONES

"As a child I wanted to be an astronaut, if not from outer space. It turned out the person who inspired me to be interested in fashion was from 'another planet': his name was Bryan Ferry of Roxy Music.

I remember the first hat I ever made was for my mother. It was a navy blue straw hat with blue and white flowers. What made it interesting was the fact that it was so classic. This is the British paradox: on one side you have punk and on the other side you have the aristocracy.

I love a boat hat and I wanted to show how to make this because it is so simple – anyone can make it, of any ability and at any age. I wanted to show that even something made out of a discarded newspaper can give you fantastic attitude… Hats speak without words. You could wear it in the bath for a glamorous pin-up photograph or you could wear it to the beach. People will always be able to find you! Fashion certainly makes life beautiful. When I worked on John Galliano's shows fifteen or twenty years ago, they were amazingly beautiful – but often I was so stressed I didn't realise it at the time… True beauty should make you dream and make your heart sing. I think that's what I love about this boat hat. The fact that it's so simple makes it very stylish, very special.

Often the nicest things are the simplest things. Some people are thinkers and some people are doers and it's always good to experience the opposite of what comes naturally to you. Get inspiration from life – not just Google!"

Make a

STEPHEN JONES FLYING BOAT HAT

YOU WILL NEED:

A thin metal clothes hanger

Strong pliers

Tape measure

Make-up sponge

Scotch-tape

Magazine or newspaper

Permanent marker pen

Ribbon or tulle (optional)

THE MAKE:

1. Use your pliers to cut off the hanger's hook and straighten the remaining wire.

2. Take your tape measure and measure the crown of your head from ear to ear – it will be around 30–34cm depending on how big your head is.

3. Now for the maths bit. With the permanent marker mark the following measurements along the wire from left to right: 4cm, half your head measurement (around 15–17cm), 1cm, your full head measurement, 1cm, and then another half head measurement. Make sure you leave some excess hanger.

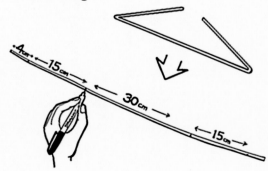

4. Do the next bit slowly and carefully, or you will end up with a lopsided hat. Using your pliers, bend the hanger into the shape of an Alice band, as shown in the picture. Start at the crown and try to fold evenly down on each side. The excess wire on the right side should swoosh up to the stars and create the spike at the top of the head.

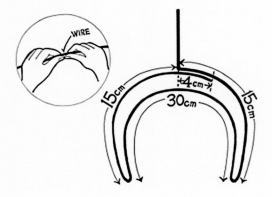

5. The 4cm at the start of the wire is where the two pieces of wire overlap. Secure these tightly together with Scotch-tape. Test it. Make sure the raw edges don't dig into your head.

6. Cut a corner of a sponge and pierce it onto the top of the spike – you want all eyes on you, not speared on the wire.

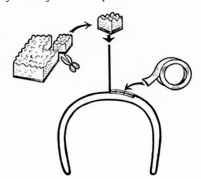

7. Now take a sheet of your favourite magazine or newspaper and fold it in half. Try to have the headline showing on the outside of the hat. Be savvy, opt for 'Celebrating Style' rather than 'What Was She Thinking?'

8. Fold the top left and right corners down to meet in the middle, then fold up the excess at the bottom towards the point at the top of the triangle. Fold this flap in on itself again to create a double layer.

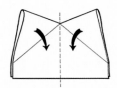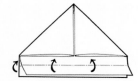

9. Now the moment of truth: put your wire frame on and carefully balance the hat over your spiked sponge. *Voila*! Your magic flying hat is ready to impress at any party. Style as your mood permits – add extra veiling or flowers, or perhaps an owl and a pussycat to float away in your boat? Most of all, enjoy!

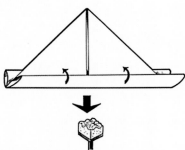

HARRODS

The Harrods Bear has delighted countless customers from all over the world. Here she wears an exclusive look and shows you 'how to'. As one of Harrods' most recognised icons, our beloved bear has rubbed shoulders with our glamorous clientele, witnessed magnificent brand takeovers and, most recently, seen the opening of the spectacular Harrods Shoe Heaven. Here, our one-of-a-kind bear has opted to wear a runway look created by one of my most favourite designers, Balmain, accessorised with an Ethan K mini croc bag, complete with one of Ethan's signature clasps, the Hedgehog. Have fun creating your chic outfit for a very chic bear!

HELEN DAVID

Make a

HARRODS
BALMAIN TEDDY BEAR

YOU WILL NEED:

Teddy bear in need of a new outfit

Thermo-sensitive pen (ink turns invisible when ironed)

Permanent fabric pen (to create the print)

Cotton jersey (and a t-shirt pattern) OR a ready-made baby tee

Leather, ideally ready-quilted

Scissors

Iron

Needle and embroidery thread or fabric glue

Diamante trim or glitter fabric glue

Sewing machine

The Houndstooth Top

THE MAKE:

1. Assess your dressmaking skills. A true couturier can copy and cut out a top without panic. However, no one will know if you skip this step and start with a baby tee.

2. Create your own houndstooth print using a thermo-sensitive pen. Cotton jersey works best here as you want something that will take the ink. Again, you can buy the fabric ready-printed and embellish on this.

3. If you are making your own top, trace your pattern templates onto the reverse side of your houndstooth fabric, then cut out and sew together.

4. Add the diamante trim (or glitter fabric glue) to set off the edge of the houndstooth print.

5. *Voila*, a Balmain outfit fit for the front row, or this fashion bear.

The Matelassé Skirt

THE MAKE:

1. Measure round your teddy bear's waist, and down to her toes, and adjust the pattern on p. 219 to fit your bear (this bear has a 42cm waist and measures 10cm waist to toe).

2. Once you have copied and cut out the pattern pieces, place them on the reverse side of the leather and cut out according to the quantity specified on each pattern piece.

3. Draw a circle on a piece of paper that measures the same circumference as teddy's waist, then lay out your cut leather pieces, face-down. To create the folds and pleats you need to follow the pieces around the circle (see p. 219), then stitch them together.

4. When the skirt is complete, don't forget to cut and stitch a lining to the underside of the skirt. The devil is in the detail with couture.

5. Finally, cut and fold a strip of quilted leather to act as the waistband, or for a touch of bling why not add a chainmail belt and make a real statement?

CHARLOTTE OLYMPIA

"From a young age I was drawn to the glamour of old Hollywood. I used to watch black and white movies with my mother and try on her shoes; she had a wonderful collection of Manolos. My grandmother, Zehava, was a very elegant woman who inspired me to set my hair in waves and wear red lipstick. I like to dress up and enjoy making an effort whether it's a Monday morning or a Friday night.

I enjoy designing for women who like to dress from the feet up. My shoes are feminine, with a modern silhouette and a touch of humour. Shoes are very sculptural, which is why I especially love the development process when designs become prototypes. Form and function are both very important. I like my shoes to look beautiful both on and off the foot and I believe they should be wearable throughout the day and into the night. Every woman has a heel height they feel comfortable in. If I am spending the day running around with my three boys, I tend to wear a pair of flats, but if I feel like conquering the world I reach for my highest heels!

I have always loved to make things – it's one of the reasons I love what I do. It's fantastic to be able to come up with a concept and then see it become a reality – why don't you give it a try?"

CHARLOTTE OLYMPIA
DOLLY SHOES

YOU WILL NEED:

Silk flowers

Pair of high heels

Glue gun

Legs that need a walk

THE MAKE:

1. Choose a bouquet of beautiful silk flowers, in different shades and styles. No one likes a stingy bouquet; the same applies to your feet.

2. Pick a pair of heels that need springtime in their step.

3. Use the glue gun and let your imagination and garden grow – start at the toes and cover the shoe.

4. Now tiptoe through the tulips!

RIFAT ÖZBEK

" I originally studied architecture at university but got somewhat distracted by the extraordinary glam rock scene, so I changed courses and went to study fashion at St Martin's School of Art.

After twenty years in fashion, the business had changed in so many ways and I felt I wanted a break. My new collection was all about cushions. I launched a shop and helped work on the interior of Robin Birley's club, 5 Hertford St.

For this project, I combined my past and my present. Handbags and shoes are the most important fashion accessory and so I thought I could easily turn one of my YASTIK cushions into the YASTIK clutch bag – certainly easier than turning it into a shoe!

For me, every cushion has its own beauty. I can't help considering them like a brooch on a dress – they are the accessory that lifts a whole room! "

Make a
RIFAT ÖZBEK
CUSHION CLUTCH

YOU WILL NEED:

Fashionable cushion cover

Brocade, brooches, epaulettes, ideas

1 large frog fastener from a haberdashery

Needle

Thread

A night out

THE MAKE:

1. Choose a cushion cover that will complement your look. Velvet is a nice option for an evening bag.

2. Fold the cushion cover in half. Ideally the concealed zip will be on the side, as you'll use this to slip your essential things in and out of the place the cushion pad once lived.

3. Choose your embellishment. Try different styles and designs: epaulettes can be fun, but choose small ones.

4. Frog fasteners are brilliant for adding a Rococo flourish as well as creating a faux close to the clutch. Attach a large frog fastener in the middle of the base of the cushion, one piece on each side of the cushion, ensuring the two sides meet and can be knotted together. If your cushion needs to lead a double life, gently tack the fastener in place, being careful not to sew through more than one layer of fabric. If you decide its life on the sofa is over, you can glue the fastenings on and the transformation will be permanent.

5. You can stop here or extend the decoration so you have a front and back to your bag. More frog fasteners can be used like Prince of Wales motifs to build a pattern on the front face of the bag, and you can add curtain tassels, brocades or velvet ribbons for straps. But a minimal design is often the best way to achieve maximum style.

6. Once your embellishments are sewn or glued into place, all you need now are the essentials – lipstick, phone, invite. Throw on your glad rags and wait for all your fashionable flapper friends to covet your cushion clutch.

VAL GARLAND AND LOLA'S CUPCAKES

> I first discovered make-up when I was four, watching my mother apply her Revlon toasty beige foundation and Elizabeth Arden matt red lipstick. She wouldn't dream of leaving the house without them. This ritual of applying a red lip immediately makes one feel glamorous, sexy and confident. It makes you feel invincible and cries 'get your face on girl and change the world!'.
>
> Here, with a glitter-red lip and a plate of cupcakes, suddenly the world and everything in it is transformed into a moment of utterly delicious abandonment.

> What makes baking beautiful is it allows you to create something spectacular and truly delicious from seemingly simple, everyday ingredients. Baking spreads a smile and brings people together. Here at LOLA's we believe in being passionate about what you do and making your creations with love – what better way to show how you feel than these (incredibly easy to make) sugar lips?

Make

VAL'S GLITTER LIPS
AND
LOLA'S SWEET SUGAR LIPS CUPCAKES

FOR VAL'S GLITTER LIPS

YOU WILL NEED:

Red lip pencil

Red lipstick

Rounded tip lip brush

Red glitter (from MAC or other professional make-up suppliers)

THE MAKE:

1. Using the lip pencil, outline your lips in a cupid bow shape.

2. Fill the insides, using the pencil, and then apply lipstick over the top using a lip brush.

3. Press red glitter on top of the lipstick with the lip brush – hold a tissue underneath your lips to prevent any glitter from falling onto your chin.

FOR LOLA'S VANILLA CUPCAKES

YOU WILL NEED:

For the sponge:

175g plain flour

1 tsp baking powder

A pinch of salt

150g soft butter, cubed

150g caster sugar

½ vanilla pod, split and seeds scraped out

3 large eggs

12 muffin cases

Electric hand whisk

For the vanilla buttercream:

120g soft butter, cubed

500g icing sugar

1 tsp vanilla extract

1 tbsp milk

Food colouring of your choice

To decorate the 'lips':

Chocolate of your choice (approx. 15g per set of lips)

Silicone lips mould(s)

Decorating paintbrush (food-safe)

Edible lustre dust (deep red, magenta and rosy pink, similar to Val's MAC shades)

Edible red and/or gold glitter

THE MAKE:

1. Pre-heat the oven to 180°C/gas mark 4.

2. Sift the flour, baking powder and salt into a bowl.

3. Put the butter and sugar into a separate bowl then beat with an electric hand whisk until pale and fluffy. Stop occasionally to scrape down the sides of the bowl with a rubber spatula.

4. Add the vanilla seeds and then the eggs to the butter and sugar, one at a time, beating well after each addition.

5. Slowly add the sifted dry ingredients and beat on a low speed until evenly combined.

6. Divide the mixture to fill your twelve muffin cases then bake in an oven for 20–25 minutes, or until well risen or a skewer inserted into the middle comes out clean. Remove from the oven and leave to cool completely on a wire rack before decorating.

7. While the cupcakes are cooling, make your buttercream. Put the butter in a bowl and beat with an electric hand whisk until very soft and smooth.

8. Sift half the sugar into the bowl, beating until incorporated. Add the vanilla and then add the remaining sugar and beat on a low speed.

9. Slowly pour in the milk and when this is mixed in beat for 3–5 minutes on a higher speed.

10. Add a few drops of the food colouring of your choice. Beat until the colour is evenly mixed and pop in the fridge until you need it.

11. Fill a piping bag fitted with a star nozzle with the coloured buttercream. Starting in the centre of the cupcake, squeeze the bag gently, piping in an anti-clockwise direction. Pipe a single ring of buttercream around the starting point, then a second circle around this to cover the surface of the cupcake. Repeat on all cupcakes.

12. Now melt the chocolate in a Pyrex bowl set over a pan of simmering water, making sure the bottom of the bowl doesn't touch the water.

13. Fill the lips mould with melted chocolate, then place in the freezer for about 10 minutes, until the chocolate has set. Repeat until you have the number of lips you want to make. You can buy several lip moulds to make batches in bulk, but if you want to make them in different colours, or flavours, then preparing each individually is best.

14. Pop the chocolate out of the mould and, taking Val's design as your inspiration, create an edible version. Warm the chocolate lips a little using your fingertip and apply lustre dust and glitter instead of make-up to 'paint' the lips. Perfect for chocolate kisses.

MARKUS LUPFER

66 When I was very young I wanted to be a chef. I didn't get into fashion until a little later in life, but throughout my childhood my glamorous grandmother was always a creative, stylish influence.

Ideas can spring from anywhere and I usually go with my gut instinct. Living in London is great – it's an amazing source and there's always something inspiring around the corner. I love it when a nice chilled Saturday afternoon with friends inspires me.

I wanted to transform an everyday jumper into something special by adding sequins and sparkle. If your favourite jumper were to get a hole – no panic! –Why not use the opportunity to get creative and repair? Keep calm and simply add sequins. It's an excellent chance to get some sparkle involved! I hope my clothes help make the wearer feel confident and special, beautiful and happy. I always try to inject a little humour into our designs as a smile can go a long way. 99

YOU WILL NEED:

A plain sweatshirt (with or without holes!)

Scissors

Piece of card

Felt-tip pen

Bondaweb

Strips of glittery ribbon and shiny fabric scraps – the more sparkle the better

Iron

TIP: When choosing glitter fabric or ribbon be sure to pick a heatproof material that won't melt when ironed. Choose similar weight fabric to your sweatshirt so the garment will lie flat, and avoid anything that may feel itchy against your skin.

1 HOLE

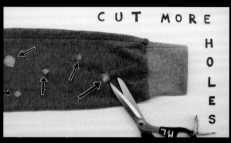

CUT MORE HOLES

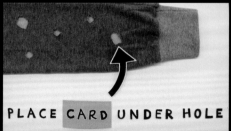

PLACE CARD UNDER HOLE

TRACE

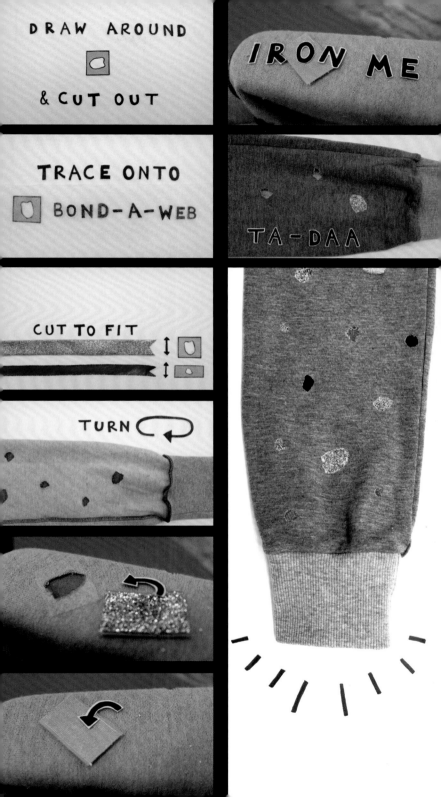

DRAW AROUND
& CUT OUT

IRON ME

TRACE ONTO
BOND-A-WEB

TA-DAA

CUT TO FIT

TURN

FRED BUTLER

I've wanted to be a fashion designer since age seven so it's just been a tunnel-vision mission ever since. I can't separate my work and my life – it's all one obsession which occupies my brain 24/7.

I'm into everything. I LOVE the crossover of all creativity. I started my blog as a platform to share the exciting experiences I was witnessing and to have an excuse to discover more. What drives me to design is the process of problem-solving. I like my pieces to function as ornaments as much as body adornments. They are cosmic structures to uplift your day whether they're hanging on the wall or round your neck.

To me, beauty in life happens when people are open. If someone is 100% non-judgemental, and open to exchange with whatever crosses their path, that is ultimate beauty. That's why I like curious accessories as a method of sparking conversation between strangers. If this world has any chance of cooperating on improvement then we need better dialogue. If we each take responsibility for our own actions and inspire those directly around us, there could be a chain reaction.

I created this alphabet candy necklace as I like playing with perceptions of accessories and jewellery. I like using unexpected materials and this is an experiment for all the family to get involved in! This project was the first I did with my assistant Amy and it was a magic bonding moment spent boiling sweets!

What makes me happy? When the sun is shining. When I'm on the back of a scooter with my dad like I was on the back of his bike when I was a kid; when I'm blissed out in Shavasana at yoga; when I'm in bed having a lie-in and the rainbow-maker is spinning spectrums in my room. Colour has always inspired me. There is a Kandinsky quote that sums up how I feel:

'Colour makes a momentary and superficial impression on a soul whose sensibility is slightly developed... But to a more sensitive soul the effect of colours is deeply and intensely moving.'

Life is beautiful in ways you never expect.

Make
FRED BUTLER
RAINBOW CANDY JEWELLERY

YOU WILL NEED:

Plain flour, for dusting

500g box 'ready-to-roll' icing

Alphabet fridge magnets, or plastic shapes, for moulding

Cling film

Clear boiled sweets, such as glacier mints (about 5 per jewel/shape)

Selection of liquid food colourings

Jump rings (or other jewellery attachments, such as earring hooks)

Coloured elastic cord or ribbon

THE MAKE:

1. Sprinkle a clean work surface with flour, and roll a good chunk of icing into a small ball about the size of a satsuma. Squash it flat to make a circular disc about 4cm deep.

2. Press your chosen plastic letter firmly into the icing to create a deep imprint. Remove the plastic shape then lay cling film over the imprinted letter, taking care to push it into all the corners so it takes a true form of the shape; this will also help you pop the sweet out later.

3. Put the plastic shape back into the mould and chill in the fridge or freezer for a few minutes to harden. Repeat the process until you have created enough moulds for all the shapes or letters you want. Once they have all hardened, remove the plastic shapes and place the cling film-covered moulds on a tray.

4. Melt the first batch of boiled sweets – take extra care at this stage! You need about 5 sweets per mould and, if you want your letters in rainbow shades, you will need to melt and dye each colour separately. Put sweets in a Pyrex bowl, then place over a saucepan with a small amount of simmering water in it.

5. Once melted, stir in a few drops of food colouring for an extra intense colour injection. Slowly pour or pipette the coloured liquid into one of the lined moulds, being very careful not to let the liquid sugar overflow.

6. Whilst the sugar is still liquid, gently drop a jump ring into the top of the letter so the necklace has something to hang from, or add a hook if you are creating earrings. Hold in place for a few seconds, so nothing vital sinks.

7. Repeat this process until all your moulds are filled, place in the fridge and leave to set – this should take an hour or so.

8. When your candy shapes feel rock hard, pop them out of the moulds and thread the coloured cord through the jump rings. Wear, eat, enjoy!

CAMBRIDGE SATCHEL COMPANY

“ I had a satchel at school and it lasted for many years, improving its looks with age. I tend to only buy things I fall in love with and I want to keep for a long time. Our satchels were created from a desire to step away from a disposable society and have fewer but lovelier things.

Inspiration comes from beautiful things – plants, flowers, open spaces, dogs and horses… oh, and colour, lots of colour! I love creating and making things – it's a treat to put time aside to create something, whether it's a garden border or a batch of Welsh cakes. This felt satchel Kindle cover is a fun project that makes me smile. Always find time to sit down and read a book, or a Kindle pulled from this felt satchel! ” JULIE DEANE

Make a
CAMBRIDGE SATCHEL COMPANY
KINDLE COVER

YOU WILL NEED:

Kindle/tablet device

Pencil

Paper

Ruler/measuring tape

Scissors

Tracing paper

Bondaweb, at least 100 x 80cm

2 pieces of orange felt, at least 50cm square

Piece of red felt, at least 30cm square

Piece of pink felt, at least 30cm square

Cotton lining fabric, enough to cover all the felt

Sewing machine

Needle

Thread or embroidery thread (3 colours to match the felt colours plus pale grey)

Pins

2 x 12mm D-ring buckles

Sharpie pen

Iron

This has been designed to fit around your Kindle, but you can adapt this to create covers for any of your devices.

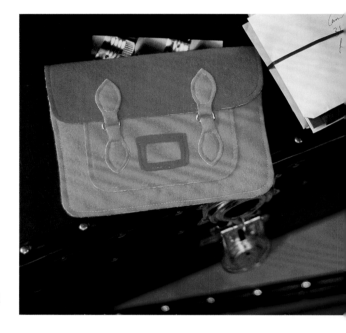

THE MAKE:

1. Create a pattern by drawing around your Kindle on paper then measure an extra 1cm and cut around the larger outline. Next create paper templates for the straps and cardholder and cut these out.

2. Before you cut your felt pieces, use Bondaweb to fuse a piece of lining fabric to each of your felt squares, ironing the three layers together. This will strengthen your fabric and give you a clean line when you cut it.

3. Place the Kindle template onto a square of felt, mark around the outline and cut out. Repeat using the other felt squares. You want to cut two orange pieces to form the main body of the bag, one piece of red to create the flap and one piece of pink for the front pocket. Cut out four straps from the orange felt, and then the cardholder in the red felt.

4. Stitch around the edge of each felt Kindle shape. Try to sew close to the edge, about 1cm in from the border, using a matching coloured thread to define your outline or, to be totally authentic to the Cambridge Satchel Company design, use a light grey.

5. Place the pink Kindle-shaped piece onto the orange to create the front pocket of the bag. Measure carefully so that the pink felt is 3cm from the side edge and 2cm from the bottom edge of the orange piece.

6. Pin and tack carefully around the edge of the pink that lies on top of the orange and cut off the excess pink felt.

7. Now turn the orange over so that you have the back/lined orange side towards you and place the red felt Kindle shape here. Place the long bottom length of the red rectangle felt piece about 9cm up from the bottom edge of the matching side of the orange rectangle. The rest will fold over the top, and behind the orange felt, to create the faux flap for your satchel; pin

and tack in place. Next, flip the satchel back over and sew around the front pocket through all three layers.

8. Now to add the straps and real character of the bag. First, place the lower straps and D-ring in place as shown. Measure so the straps are 1.5cm from the bottom of the pink pocket and 1.5cm from the side edge of it. Pin and tack these down. Place the cardholder 1.5cm from the bottom of the pink pocket. Now position the top straps on the red flap, check the straps meet, then pin and tack into place using the light grey sewing thread.

9. Thread the top straps through the D-ring in the bottom straps and sew these all in place by hand.

10. Final flourish, for those using a machine: top stitch 0.5cm from the edge in grey, over the colour-coordinating outline you sewed earlier. If using a machine for this project it is best to sew two layers like this to really define the outline; if you're hand-stitching you only need stitch one outline in the grey. Last job – sew the remaining orange felt to the back of the completed front piece to finish your cover. Leave an opening for your Kindle to slip into by sewing about 8cm from the top edge. Your mini satchel is now complete and you've given modern technology some old-school charm.

CHINTI AND PARKER

"We started Chinti and Parker with one very clear objective: to create pieces we wanted to wear. The first capsule collection was just thirty pieces – they were a timeless, consciously manufactured range of basics. Each season since we've expanded on our original philosophy.

I have always loved design – from interior to fashion – and have always had a strong view on what I like. Rachel and I always dreamt of working together – we knew we would work well as a team because our aesthetics are so similar. It used to be a joke that we dressed the same and accidentally bought the same pieces, but it ended up leading to us spotting a gap in the market.

For this project we wanted to create a motif that was classic and timeless but imbued with personality. There is something nostalgic and charming about the star and, over time, it became a cornerstone of our collections.

Inspiration can come from the most unexpected of places, but for us it tends to be something that has significance and rings some sort of emotional bell. For instance, a blouse of my grandmother's or a tile pattern I saw on holiday. It can be very ephemeral too. The designers and I look at patterns and colours and abstract photography, as there are sometimes echoes of the way the intarsia patterns of our knitwear are formed.

Finding and discovering beauty can really bring joy to every day. Appreciating the loveliness of something leads to happiness and, although they are not intrinsically linked, happiness is beautiful." ANNA SINGH

CHINTI AND PARKER
STAR STITCHED SWEATER

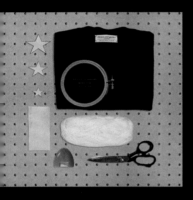

YOU WILL NEED:

Paper star templates in various sizes

Navy cashmere sweater

Chalk marker

Embroidery paper

Embroidery hoop

Cream cotton yarn or wool

Sharp darning needle

Scissors

THE MAKE:

1. Arrange star templates on the sweater and chalk around them.

2. Place embroidery paper on the underside of your sweater, behind the chalk star, and place the embroidery hoop around it. The embroidery hoop will keep the knit taut and flat while you sew, and the embroidery paper will act as a base for your stitches. The hoop will also help ensure you only stitch through one side of the jumper.

3. Thread the yarn onto the needle and using backstitch (keeping the stitch lengths as even as possible) sew all the way around the outline making sure that the tips of the star are nice and pointy.

4. Once the outline is complete fill the star with more backstitches. Start at the top and be careful to stagger your stitches to achieve an even coverage. Do not remove the embroidery hoop until you have carefully cast off, then move onto the next star.

5. For the final touch, don't forget to add your initials – Chinti-style!

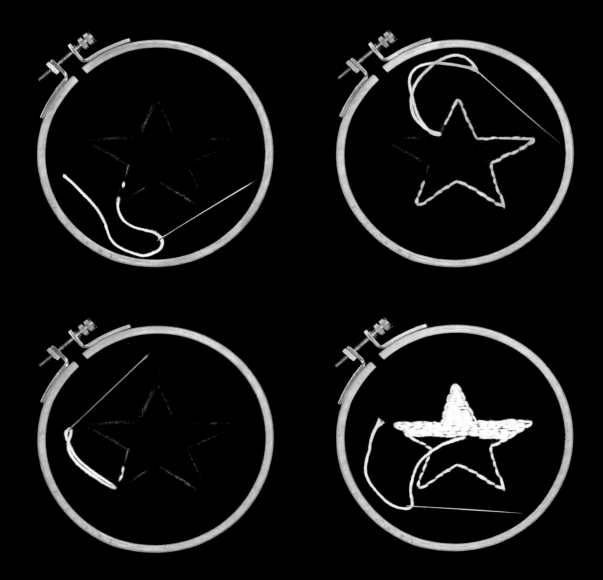

TOPSHOP

"It is important to stand out and put your own stamp on style in the fashion world. Customising allows you to be the designer and to create something unique to you. All you need is a T-shirt or pair of jeans, some ideas and a sewing kit and you will be surprised by what you can achieve."

KATE PHELAN

Make a

TOPSHOP
SWEET HEART T-SHIRT

YOU WILL NEED:

Pink fabric dye

Bowl or bucket

Rubber gloves or wooden spoon

Plain white T-shirt

Heat transfer paper with some small hearts printed onto it

Scissors

Iron

THE MAKE:

1. To make T-shirt transfers you simply need access to a computer and a printer. You can either design or draw your own heart and scan it or photograph it with your phone, or use something you find online. Be creative in your quest. Once you have the love heart on your computer, copy and paste it so you end up with multiple images, then print them onto T-shirt transfer paper.

2. Mix pink dye into a bowl or bucket filled with approximately 3 litres of water. Make it as deep or diluted as you desire, and stir well to ensure the colour is even. Best to wear rubber gloves or use a long wooden spoon so you don't dye your hands.

3. Dip just the hem into the bucket of dye until it's around 15–20cm submerged and leave the rest hanging over the side for 10 minutes. Rinse off in cold water, taking care not to splash the snow-white top of the tee, then hang to dry.

4. Now to add the love. Place the T-shirt on a flat surface and position the heart shapes facing down, cutting a square around each shape on the transfer grid. Start with the back side of the T-shirt, scatter more hearts at the hem and less towards the shoulders and chest.

5. Once all the hearts are placed on the T-shirt, carefully use the iron to press them down. It will take approximately 10 minutes on a high heat to fuse the hearts in place. Now repeat the process on the front of the T-shirt.

6. Wait for the hearts to cool down, then peel off the backing paper. Remember – do not iron directly onto the hearts once the backing paper has been removed. You will need to hand-wash these T-shirts and iron them inside out!

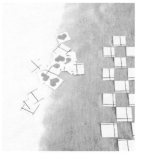

MARIAN NEWMAN
AND JULIE VERHOEVEN

" I believe nails need to be fun. It should be very much a personal love affair and nothing to do with trends. They are ten little accessories and they don't have to match anything unless you want them to. You just need to notice them and smile.

Having seen Julie's illustration, I was inspired to create my 'finger feet', so that her four fantastical ladies could be brought to life and dance! " MARIAN NEWMAN

MARIAN NEWMAN
AND JULIE VERHOEVEN
FINGER FEET

MISS PEARLY

YOU WILL NEED:

Full cover tips

Your choice of 2 or 3 pale colours

Flat backed tiny pearls (from a craft shop)

Tweezers or Blu Tac

Topcoat

Tiny beads in various colours

Cotton

Nail glue

2 fingers and Miss Pearly illustration

Card (to mount illustration)

THE MAKE:

*Miss Pearly is clearly a lover of beautiful things!
I based the nail design on a traditional 'pearly
queen' costume but added flying beads to enhance
her dancing. Think of an amazing Tiffany lamp
with coloured light and reflective beaded fringes.*

1. Cut out and mount the Miss Pearly
   illustration on card and cut out the two
   holes at the base of the illustration.

2. Take two 'full cover' tips for two new 'feet'.

3. Take two or three colours that work with
   the Pearly Lady illustration and apply onto
   the nail tips. Paint one nail at a time so you
   can blend the colours while the polish is
   still very wet.

4. Apply flat backed pearls with tweezers or
   Blu Tac into a layer of wet top coat.
   Fashion in the style of traditional 'pearly
   kings and queens' pattern.

5. Thread tiny beads onto strands of cotton
   and glue to the back of the nail tips.

6. Attach tips to fingers with glue, slip fingers
   through the holes and watch her pearly
   beads fly as she dances.

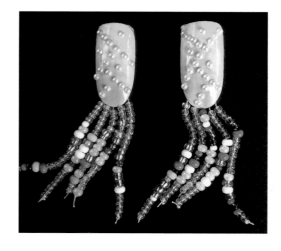

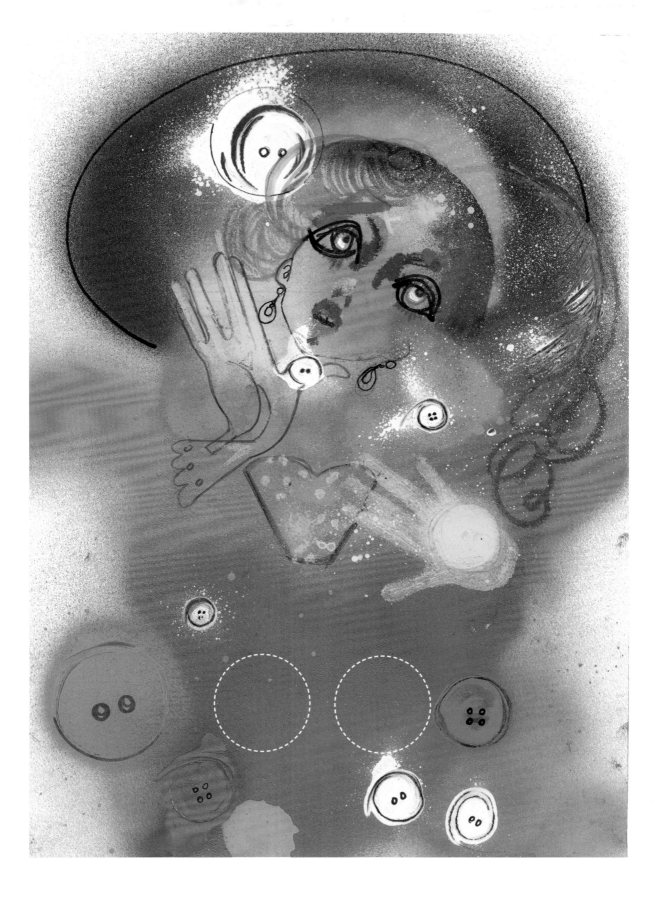

MISS FAIRY

YOU WILL NEED:

Clear full cover tips

Emery board

Pink and white polish

Holographic glitter topcoat

Faux lace

Holographic glitter

Angelina fusible fibre

Scissors

Nail glue

Pieces of clear plastic or cling film

2 fingers and the Miss Fairy Illustration

Card (to mount illustration)

THE MAKE:

Miss Fairy is a whimsical character, surrounded by sprites and fairy dust! Her world is up in the heavens and full of wonderful thoughts. Her finger feet are transparent but throw off light by way of beautiful, holographic colours. If her 'feet' were dancing there would be a sprinkle of fairy dust in her wake.

1. Cut out and mount Miss Fairy on card.

2. Use clear tips to create something more 'ethereal' and lightly shape them into an elegant long curve.

3 . Paint the tips as shown using a blend of white and holographic glitter polish at the base of the nail, working down to an opaque pink at the top to cover the natural nail underneath.

4. Apply 'Faux lace' over some of the nail and cover this with glitter. Faux lace is a type of double-sided sticky tape that, once applied, can be rubbed to make lace-like patterns to which glitter can then be stuck.

5. Using Angelina (fusible fibre, available from most craft shops), cut out some tiny wings to be applied to the sides of the nails.

6. Keep the tip of the nail clear. Behind this place a plastic backing to form a cavity and fill with holographic glitter.

7. Attach tips to fingers and slide fingers into place on illustration. Just before she starts to can-can, pierce some holes in the plastic and watch her spread a little 'fairy dust'.

MISS FASHION

YOU WILL NEED:

Full cover tips

Emery board

Clear or shimmery topcoat

Small paintbrush or eyeshadow brush

2 coloured pigments (MAC do a vast variety)

Dark polish

Embellishments (craft shop)

Nail glue

2 fingers and the Miss Fashion illustration

Card (to mount illustration)

THE MAKE:

Fashionista was a tricky one to relate to 'finger feet'! She needed to be GORGEOUS and at the cutting edge of a 'statement' fashion look! I felt Fashionista needed to be a shoe obsessive. She wears fabulous stilettos and draws attention to her shoes by wearing a seamed stocking that make her 'legs' look divine!

1. Cut out and mount Miss Fashion on card.

2. Shape your cover tips to echo that of the lower part of the leg. Fashion a nice shapely calf.

3. Shoe shopping. Marian used specially made metal appliqué stilettos but be creative – shoe pendants, lockets, sequins or sugar decorations will all work.

4. Apply topcoat and while this is still sticky (not wet) take your small brush and, very gently, press the pigments into the surface. Wipe your brush on a tissue and gently brush off any excess pigment.

5. Next, with a very light touch, apply another layer of topcoat to seal the pigment in. For an extra element lightly spray on pink pigment on one side of the tips and a blue on the other. The colour will be very faint but the changes will show as she dances.

6. Paint a thin dark stripe down one edge of the tips to give the impression of a seamed stocking.

7. Glue the stilettos onto the tip ends and attach the finger feet to your nails. Slip fingers through the illustration then it's time for Miss Fashionista to strut her stuff.

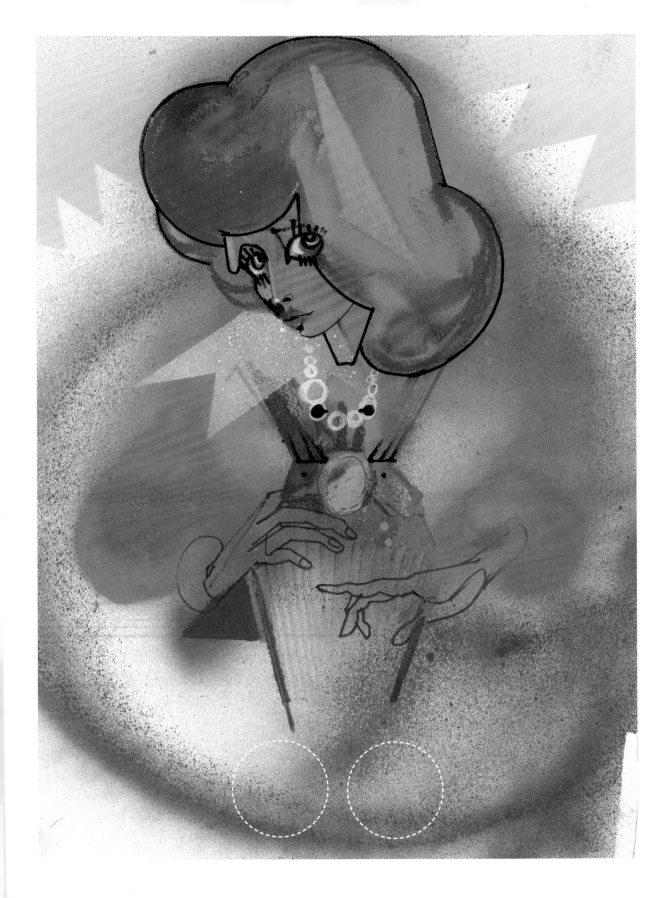

VICKI SARGE

"To make something beautiful you have to want to wear it every day yourself; it has to come from an honest place. Life and work can get stressful and difficult so I feel so fortunate that every day I go into work I am able to be creative.

When making something, originality is the key. I've always crocheted and embroidered but I only started to take it seriously when I helped a friend for his fashion show. We couldn't find any jewellery we liked so we decided to make our own crystals and appliqué them to suede! I think the best things happen organically, and I was lucky – everyone loved our take on crystals and my hand-crafted jewellery was a success from the start.

I am constantly looking at films, magazines and art for inspiration. My muse is a constantly revolving door – we all have different moods to explore and I hope my jewellery lets a woman live out her fantasies. We are bombarded by so much information these days but my inspiration often comes when I feel calm. You need to clear your head and be still or enjoy a long walk in nature, away from your phone.

This project was inspired by a piece we originally created for Mario Testino for his Alta Mode project in Peru. Pom-poms are a great way to transform something that may have seen better days into something with a bit more personality – plus pom-poms always evoke such a happy feeling that it makes the pieces feel really fun and modern. The trick with jewellery is trial and error: be brave and just give it a go!"

Make a

VICKI SARGE
POM-POM NECKLACE

YOU WILL NEED:

2 old necklaces (preferably with chain links and pendant details)

Wire-cutter pliers (or something strong enough to cut metal!)

Wool, ribbon or thick thread

Scissors

A selection of mini and large pom-poms in various colours (you can buy them in strings by the metre or create your own)

Glue gun

Wool in a selection of colours, textures, yarn width

Cardboard (if you're making your own pom-poms)

Ribbon

THE MAKE:

1. Find two necklaces and cut off the pendant detail from one using your wire-cutter pliers – you will be adding this later to the second necklace.

2. Cut a length of thread, ribbon or wool, and attach it to the pendant as neatly as possible by threading it through the eyelets or chain links, and tie with a slipknot.

3. Now take the other necklace and, with the thread you cast on, use the links of the necklace or beads (depending on the design of your necklace) to weave the two together, and tie to secure.

4. Cut the string of mini pom-poms so you have individual balls and, using your glue gun, attach them across the necklace.

5. Knot the larger pom-poms onto your necklace – these will be the focal point of your piece and should be positioned near the base.

6. Use the wire-cutter pliers to trim the ends of the necklace to about 10cm either side of your pom-pom pendant and replace with two lengths of ribbon that fit the piece round your neck, and your piece is ready to wear.

CLEMENTS RIBEIRO

"Suzanne and I met at St Martin's in London. We have always been remarkably different from each other, from our backgrounds (I'm Brazilian, she is thoroughly English), to our demeanours (I'm quiet and introspective, while she is expansive and electric), to our tastes (I was into Christian Lacroix while she was into Yohji Yamamoto). What we have in common, however, always mattered more: an intense curiosity, an omnivorous appetite for

the artistic, and a thirst for the raw and the sophisticated combined. The romance of the Bohemian life was always there to cement the bond: the thrill of making something beautiful out of limited resources.

The first collections we created entirely by ourselves, relishing the improvisation and the creative solutions that emerged from bridging our competing ideas. We are never happier than when under the spell of the creative gesture; when, deep into the process, your hand seems to know what to do next, before

you've made a conscious decision. This was never more true than with our embroideries, where we created exquisite things out of unexpected, 'poor' materials. We love working with 'found materials'. Besides the obvious benefit of recycling, found elements spike our imagination and add another creative layer.

The cat embroidery is one such layered design. Cats have always figured in our collections. The arrival of our British Blue cats, Toulouse and Marie, triggered the creative process of the entire collection. The key design in the collection was an evening dress in heavy silk georgette and panne velvet, which was to have the two cats embroidered on its top. To avoid it looking too cute we considered all sorts of solutions, settling in the end for zip tapes, which bring an unexpected 'industrial' touch to the precious materials and delicate execution; and jet buttons for eyes, which turned something beautiful and rare into something quirky. In other words: quintessential Clements Ribeiro!" INACIO RIBEIRO

Make a
CLEMENTS RIBEIRO
CAT T-SHIRT

YOU WILL NEED:

Pencil

Bondaweb

Black fabric (felt, velvet, mohair or fun fur)

Scissors

Plain T-shirt or sweatshirt

Iron

Short black zip with metal teeth

Needle and thread

Pins

Two vintage buttons for eyes (jet buttons are great)

Black embroidery thread (or other fancy thread)

Sewing machine

THE MAKE:

1. Draw or trace a cat template onto Bondaweb and stick it onto your black cat fabric – if using velvet or fur be sure to place the Bondaweb on the reverse/non-furry side. Cut around your feline outline to create the cat shape. Elongate her limbs, streamline her figure, emphasise the curve of her tail and sharpen her ears – not claws – to make her unique. Don't forget the image will flip to mirror when you iron on top.

2. Once your silhouette is finessed, gently peel off the Bondaweb layer on the fabric and press down on the T-shirt to ensure it's stuck in place.

3. Iron the Bondaweb and fabric cat so the heat fixes it to your T-shirt, being careful not to use steam. Secure it by sewing around the edges as neatly as you can.

4. Now for the clever bit – the eyes. Cut your short zip into four parts. To create the undersides of the eye, sew a simple running stitch above the zip's teeth and gently pull the thread to shape it. Repeat for the other eye.

5. Take the shaped bits of zip that create the underside of the eyes and pin in position. Allowing space for the button pupil, pin the zip 'eyelids', allowing a bit of 'lift' to add a 3D effect.

6. You can fix the two parts of the eye zips together at the corners before applying them to the T-shirt, making sure they look identical and line up. Place the eye zips on your cat and stick or sew in place – be careful though: if you sew the whole length the 'lid' will stick out too much.

7. Now place the buttons in the middle of the eyes. Vintage jet buttons add a nice focus. This cat has shank button eyes. Sew firmly in position.

8. Last touch: the whiskers. All pussycats need these. Simply hand-sew long stitches with a fancy thread – here we used black synthetic raffia – and secure them at intervals with hold stitches. Puurrfect!

SUZANNAH

"I have always been aware of fashion. According to my mum, I made my first skirt – well, a floral circle with a piece of elastic through the waistband – when I was five years old. Something must have stuck, as I still love a fifties silhouette! I grew up in a village in the north east of England and in my late teens I became obsessed with vintage clothing. I loved the way it allowed me to imagine another woman's life. There was one vintage shop in Hull old town and one in Leeds town centre where I used to buy a lot of my clothes. I would get them home and take them apart or adapt them to go out in. I didn't want to wear clothes that were the same as everyone else so I started to create 'looks' for myself, and it grew from there! I love the art of creating a piece that is beautiful at every angle and flattering at every turn. I love transforming something old into something modern, preserving the spirit of the original idea yet translating it into something new.

Inspiration is everywhere. Encourage yourself to indulge your senses and feast on what inspires you. Is it the grains of wood, the texture of flower petals or the intensity of colour in a flower market? Sit outside a cafe in an area of the world that makes you feel good and just watch and absorb; visit galleries, look at architecture, the garden, artisan bakeries, antique shops and markets, like the wonderful Porte de Clignancourt in Paris or Columbia Road and Portobello in London. The colours and invention and constant evolution of life make it beautiful."

Make a
SUZANNAH
VINTAGE DRESS

YOU WILL NEED:

Vintage dress

Scissors

Sewing machine, or Wonderweb

Full net skirt

Diamante trim, 4m

Silver coloured fine chain, 4m

Pins

Soft black leather, enough for a strip around the waist, 2.5cm wide, and two rectangles of 15 x 11cm

Wadding – two strips of 15 x 3cm

1 reel of thread and hand-sewing needle

Black zipper

Flexible glue

Black leather ribbon, for bow tie

Black grosgrain ribbon, 5cm wide, and enough for a strip around the waist

THE MAKE:

1. Find a vintage fifties day dress: go to your favourite markets, charity shops and vintage sales or search online.

2. Shorten. Cut and give your dress a fresh crisp hem; double turn for those in the know, though Wonderweb works a treat too.

3. Plump up the volume by adding fresh tulle underskirts.

4. Drape chains and diamante strips as shown (using pins to position them) to create a necklace. This shape follows the same line as a Peter Pan collar for ultimate vintage chic.

5. Add an edge with a modern leather bow. Cut a leather rectangle, pinch in the middle and glue on a neat oblong to create the centre.

6. Take two strips of leather and wadding and sew together, folding and gluing the edges to create neat rectangles. Tack these straight onto the shoulders to create tabs to 'trap' the chains, neaten the finish, and give the dress some structure. Remember – the stronger the shoulder, the smaller the waist!

7. Underarm update. Unpick the underarm area downwards at the side seam (vintage armholes are notoriously high and small). Create a modern roll back as if on a T-shirt. Roll and tack in place with simple hand-stitch.

8. Zip it. Either keep the original zip hidden for a 'climb in' option or unpick the old one and lay on a crisp new exposed zipper. Glue or machine/hand-sew this zipper tape to either side on the open back of the dress. Chunky zips add a contrasting feature to the back and can be embellished by adding lengths of chain or ribbon to the zip puller (you can use an old necklace and simply clasp it onto the puller) to create a seductive back opening.

9. Cinch the waist and emphasise curves with a layered ribbon strip. Place the leather strip over the grosgrain ribbon, and attach to the waistline with Wonderweb or a simple running stitch.

10. Dress to impress. Find or create a date. Complete the look with a fabulous up do, a bright pink lip stain and, of course, a pair of towering heels!

SAM McKNIGHT

I like doing things with my hands: hair, gardening, baking. When I do hair I like to use my hands more than tools, to make the hair look very natural. There's something about that physical connection that makes things beautiful. When I am shooting or at the shows, every minute is frenetic. I love it but you need a balance, so the solitude and calm I find in my garden and kitchen help me relax.

And, unlike gardening, the wonderful thing about baking is that it isn't dependent on the weather!

For me, cooking doesn't have to be perfect – it's more about the process and creating something. I put the same attention to detail into my baking as I would any of my work. These shortbraids combine elements of many things I love and should have a sweet sense of humour to them.

Make

SAM McKNIGHT
SHORTBRAIDS

YOU WILL NEED:

110g caster sugar, plus extra for dusting

225g butter

395g plain flour

50g cornflour

Rolling pin

Milk, to brush

THE MAKE:

1. Pre-heat the oven to 170°C/gas mark 3. Cream sugar and butter together in a large bowl until light and fluffy.

2. Measure out the flour and cornflour and sieve together as you fold into the butter and sugar. Mix thoroughly but do not over-mix – just like over-styling with too much product, it's all about balance.

3. Tip onto a lightly floured work surface and lightly knead until a dough is formed. Roll or pat out the dough so it's 1.25cm thick.

4. Draw a braid on a piece of paper that you will use as your template: you can either make one or two braids, or smaller bite-sized braids.

5. Rolling the dough/braid to your desired length, scallop around the edge and use a small sharp knife to draw in the details of the braided hair. Be careful not to cut too deep into the dough or to make the ends too wispy else they will snap off.

6. Use the side of the knife to soften the edges and create the plait detail in the dough and don't forget to finish with either an iced bow or a shortbread bow to style.

7. Brush with a little milk if desired, and transfer your braids onto a lightly greased baking sheet using a large kitchen palette knife.

8. Pop in the oven for about 15–20 minutes. Just as you would when getting your hair coloured, keep an eye on how they are doing – be sure to catch them just before they go too golden brown. Shortbread baking tones may vary according to the oven so attention to bake is necessary. Light is good; brown means overdone!

9. Leave to cool on a wire rack and dust with sugar, then put the kettle on.

NICK KNIGHT

> I have always loved the calm and beauty of afternoon tea. A delicious ritual where everyone is brought together in an informally precise ceremony that combines social interaction and an elegant visual language, expressed in delicate porcelain.

Make a
NICK KNIGHT
PERFECT CUP OF TEA

YOU WILL NEED:

Kettle

Teapot

Water

Tea

Cup and saucer

Milk

Sugar, to taste

THE MAKE:

1. Boil the kettle.

2. Warm the pot.

3. Put tea into warmed pot, immediately followed by boiling water.

4. Making tea is a chemical reaction. It has to take place in exact conditions… so it is vital that the water is 100°C.

5. Allow pot to stand for 4½ minutes while the tea brews.

6. Choose a teacup. This is a sensory experience as well as a social one so consider how the porcelain will feel against the lips – the more delicate the better.

MANOLO BLAHNIK

" Fashion is about having fun, being a bit
crazy and original – so let it be with biscuits
and Blahniks and life will be beautiful! "

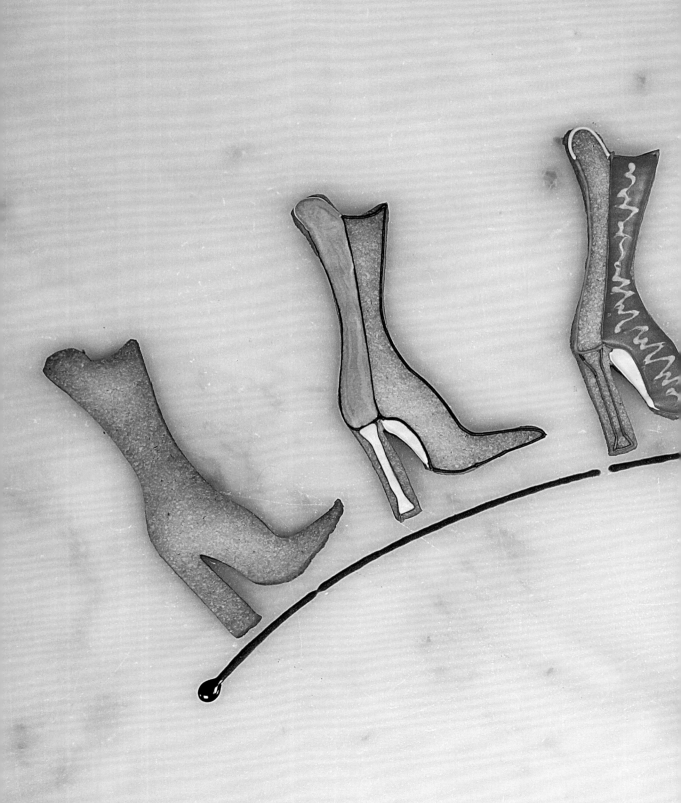

MANOLO BLAHNIK
BISCUITS

BLAHNIK BOOTS

YOU WILL NEED:

180g unsalted butter, plus extra for greasing

70g icing sugar

230g flour

20g cocoa powder

20g egg white (roughly equivalent to the white of 1 small egg, or half the white from 1 large egg)

20g melted butter

Icing, in shades of your choice

Electric mixer, like a KitchenAid

Cling film

Baking parchment

Boot template

Baking tray

THE MAKE:

1. Using a small electric mixer, with a paddle attachment, make a crumble with the butter, icing sugar, flour and cocoa powder.

2. Add the egg white followed by gently melted butter.

3. Mix until thoroughly combined, wrap in cling film and leave to chill in the fridge for 30 minutes to an hour. Preheat the oven to 180°C/gas mark 4

4. Unwrap the dough and roll out between 2 sheets of baking parchment to a thickness of ½ cm, then remove the top sheet.

5. Trace silhouette of boot onto a clean sheet of baking parchment and use this as a template, placing it over the pastry and cutting around the paper shape with a knife. Repeat – be sure to make boots in pairs.

6. Line your dough boots on a greased or lined baking tray, ensuring that they're spaced well apart.

7. Bake for 6 minutes, then turn the tray around and bake for a further 2 minutes or until golden, and leave to cool for a few minutes.

8. Ice in Blahnik-style shades, leaving the laces till last.

Some of these quantities might seem odd. Trust us.
The recipe was created by the Head Pastry Chef at the
Berkeley Hotel's Prêt-à-Portea and he modifies the
ingredients so biscuits keep their shape when baking.

BISCUIT BUCKLES

YOU WILL NEED:

225g soft unsalted butter, plus extra for greasing

140g caster sugar

1 egg yolk

2 tsp vanilla extract

280g plain flour

A pinch of salt

Cling film

Baking parchment

5cm round pastry cutter

Icing, silver balls and edible glitter

Baking tray

THE MAKE:

1. Pre-heat the oven to 180°C/gas mark 4. Add butter and sugar to a bowl and mix well with a wooden spoon, then beat in the egg yolk and vanilla extract.

2. Sift in the flour and add a pinch of salt then mix until thoroughly combined. Shape the dough into a ball and wrap in cling film. Leave to chill in the fridge for 30 minutes to an hour.

3. Unwrap the dough and roll out between two sheets of baking parchment until ½ cm thick. Remove the top sheet and, using a circular pastry cutter, cut ten pieces, the shape of buckles, then carefully place them on a greased or lined baking tray, making sure they're well spaced out.

4. Bake for 7 minutes, until a light golden colour.

5. When sufficiently cool, fashion your biscuits into buckles by adding icing, silver balls, edible glitter and your imagination.

6. Serve with tea or add clear varnish and a clip to the reverse, attach to your shoe and wear into the night.

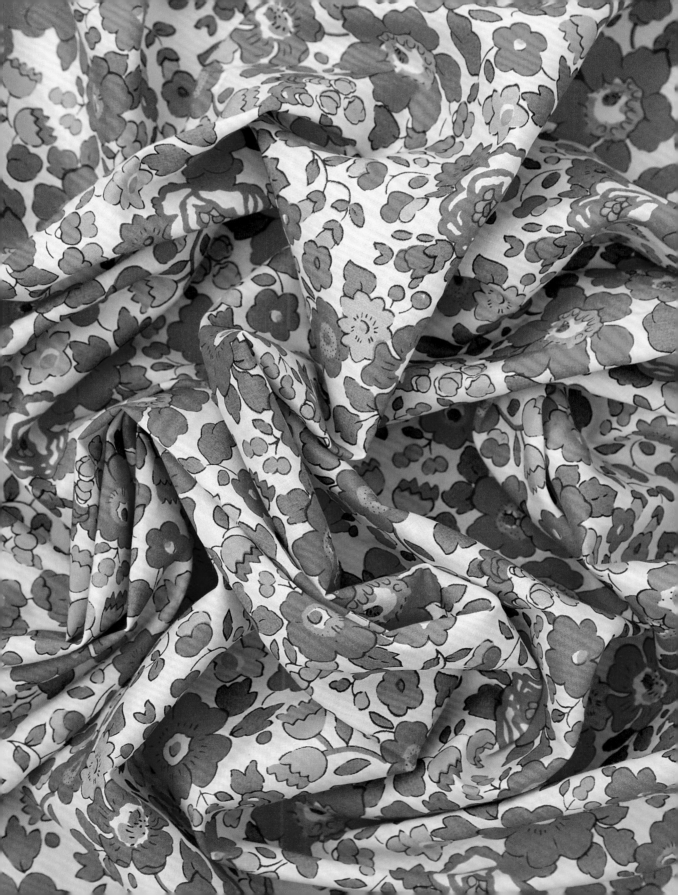

LIBERTY

Arthur Liberty, founder of the London emporium, said,
'I was determined not to follow fashion but to create new
ones.' This pioneering spirit led him to travel the world looking for
individual pieces to inspire his clientele. The store opened in 1875
stocking ornaments, art fabrics and objets d'art from the East and
continues to showcase the unique and unexpected but always the
most beautiful. As Oscar Wilde said, 'Liberty is the chosen resort of
the artistic shopper.'

Treat yourself to some Liberty art fabric and create something
useful from something special.

Make a
LIBERTY
OVEN MITT

YOU WILL NEED:

2 pieces of 60 x 80cm Liberty-print fabric (Liberty used Betsy Print)

2 pieces of 60 x 80cm plain cream fabric

1 piece of 60 x 40cm heat-resistant wadding

Water-soluble fabric marker pen

1m Liberty-print bias binding (Liberty used Pepper Print)

Sewing machine

Co-ordinating colour thread

Scissors

Needle, thread, sewing kit

THE MAKE:

1. Cut your fabric so you have two 60 x 80cm rectangles in Liberty print, two pieces measuring 60 x 80cm in plain fabric, and one 60 x 40cm rectangle of heat-resistant wadding.

2. Mark criss-cross diagonal lines onto the right side of one of the Liberty fabric pieces with a water-soluble fabric pen.

3. Layer the fabric into a sandwich like so: Liberty print, plain fabric, wadding, plain fabric, Liberty print.

4. Make sure the right sides are facing out (i.e. the Liberty print should be facing outwards), then pin together at the edges.

5. Sew the sandwich together following the direction of the diagonal lines.

6. Now rotate and sew along the other lines to make a criss-cross pattern.

7. Copy and cut out the oven mitt pattern template to size. Then flip over the template and cut out a second mitt.

8. Cut 20cm of bias binding.

9. Fold it in half along the length as shown and match the edges together and then sew along the open edge. Fold in half the other way and press. Put aside, as this will form your oven mitt hanging loop.

10. Cut 2 x 25cm strips of the same bias binding. Fold one piece along the bottom edge of one of the mitts and sew into place so it covers the raw edge.

11. Complete on both mitts.

12. Take your hanging loop and pin into place as shown. Match the right (front) sides together and pin in place. The hanging loop will be inside the mitt for now.

13. Sew around the outside of one mitt, leaving a 1.5cm seam allowance.

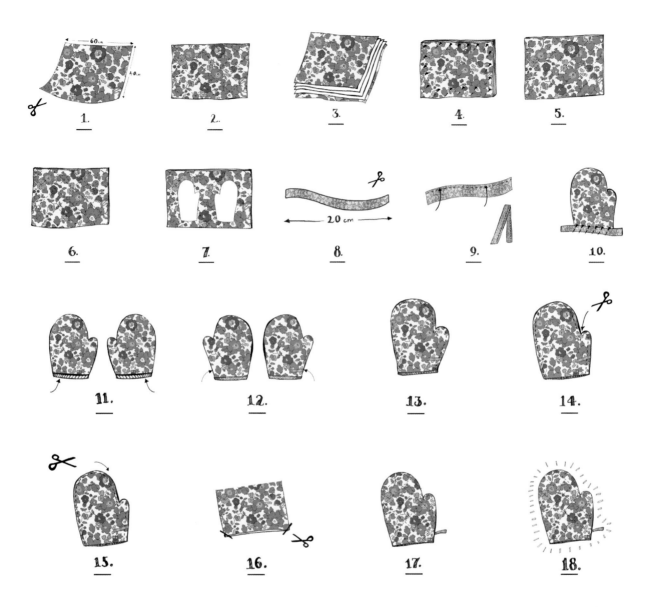

14. Carefully snip into the corner between the fingers and thumb area, careful not to cut into the stitch line.

15. Trim any excess seam allowance from around the glove to neaten. This will ensure it's not too bulky when you turn it the right way round.

16. Snip the corners of the bottom off at an angle.

17. Turn the mitt the right way out.

18. Press all the seams to neaten them up and get cooking!

ROLAND MOURET

"Cooking is like fashion, it's a shared moment. For me, as the son of a butcher, the two are related: fashion for clothes and cooking for food, for life. Here's an easy way to customise a dress and give it a second life. Be as creative with your apron as you are in the kitchen."

Make a

ROLAND MOURET
FASHION STATEMENT APRON

YOU WILL NEED:

Scissors

An old dress

Seam ripper

Grosgrain ribbon

Needle and thread

THE MAKE:

1. Remove the full back panel so just the front of your dress remains.

2. Take a piece of ribbon and stitch along the waistline, then attach ribbon at the back to form support. You can cross or position straight shoulder straps – the trick here is the wider the strap, the narrower your frame will appear.

3. Tie the ribbon in a bow and your apron is complete. Be sure to exaggerate the shoulders and cinch in the waist, as well as making sure it serves the purpose of protecting your front from any flying ingredients.

MARY McCARTNEY

"A friend of mine showed me how to make granola – until then I hadn't realised how easy it was. I love cooking because it is about touch, smell and colour. I call this version 'Grinola' because you should smile and have some fun with the recipe.

When I'm out with my camera, I love to let my mind wander and make up little stories about what I'm seeing. Similarly, when you're making this, indulge your imagination, and when the mood takes you, come up with your own flavour combinations – be sure to add all your favourite ingredients."

MARY McCARTNEY
'GRINola'

YOU WILL NEED:

4 tbsp sunflower or vegetable oil

10 tbsp maple syrup

10 tbsp runny honey

500g oats, preferably jumbo

100g Brazil nuts, chopped

100g almonds, chopped

100g raisins

100g dried apricots, chopped

2 baking trays

Airtight glass jars and/or cellophane bags and tie twists

Ribbon (optional)

Labels (optional)

THE MAKE:

1. Pre-heat the oven to 150°C/gas mark 2. Line two baking trays with greaseproof paper.

2. Mix the oil, maple syrup and honey in a small saucepan and heat gently until warm and melted together. Take care not to overheat – you don't want the mixture to boil. Remove from the heat and set aside while you prepare the dry ingredients.

3. In a large mixing bowl combine the oats and chopped nuts.

4. Drizzle the syrup over the oats and nuts and mix together thoroughly so the ingredients are well coated.

5. Spread the mixture out evenly over the baking trays. Bake for 30–40 minutes, taking the granola out of the oven every 10 minutes to move it around so that it bakes evenly.

6. When it is golden brown all over, remove from the oven. Stir in the raisins and chopped apricots. As it cools it will become lovely and crunchy.

7. Once cool, divide into small, airtight glass jars. If gifting, decorate the jars by tying around a colourful ribbon in a bow or stick on a hand-written label of love.

HERMÈS

The birth of an Hermès bag is first and foremost conditioned by the quality of the carefully selected precious material from which it will be made. Then comes the know-how of the craftsman, animated by a desire to enhance the material and achieve beauty, a story in motion. With the hand as the main player, the eye as conductor and the heart as guide, they ensure the exacting attention to detail proper to Hermès and, ultimately, to attain perfection. It is thus with a smile that Hermès proposes a composition in paper of our much loved Kelly bag.

In our workshops these inanimate objects assume a soul. They are living entities; each bag is born of one craftsman. Our hope is this: that you, craftsman of card, playing with the simple tools of paper, scissors and colour, experience in some small measure the beautiful life of our own ateliers. Ready, steady, Kelly!

Make a

HERMÈS
(PAPER) KELLY BAG

YOU WILL NEED:

Kelly template

Card or paper

Scissors

Glue

A sense of luxury

THE MAKE:

1. Carefully cut out this template.

2. Fold along the orange lines creating concertina folds on each side.

3. Cut where marked with blue lines then thread 'straps' through as indicated.

4. Apply glue to the orange dots and stick together to create your very own mini Kelly.

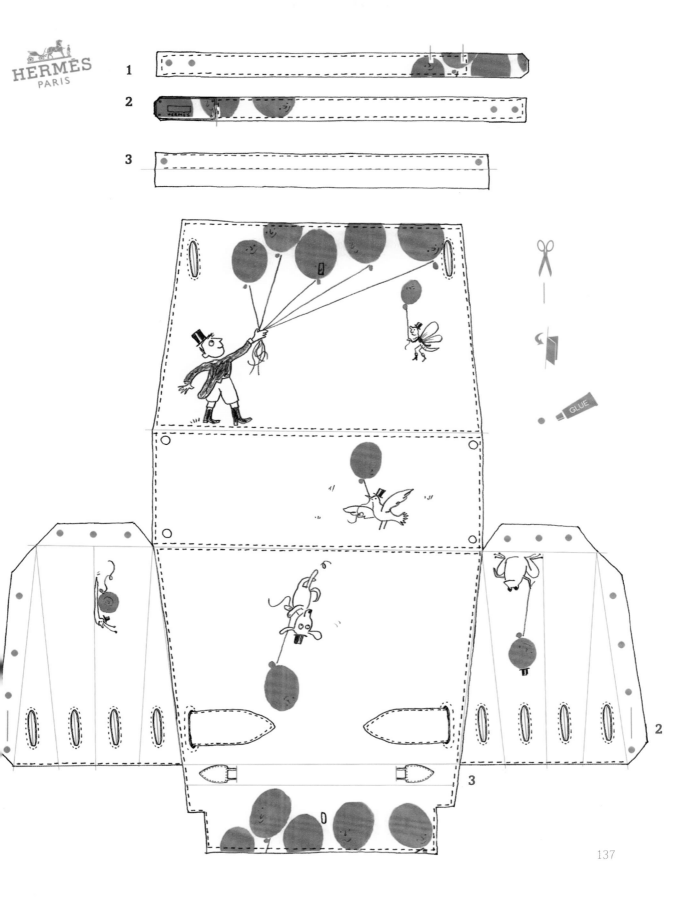

TATTY DEVINE

I find inspiration in the strangest places; the most exciting ideas come when you least expect them. Rosie and I knew we could make things happen together and started Tatty Devine almost by accident.

The most important part of making jewellery for me is making something you love and are proud of. Jewellery is so much more than the sum of its parts – it's about memory, joy and a host of other emotions. Jewellery can tell people who you are. I love the days when putting on jewellery can change your world.

I find beauty in the creativity of humans, from the strange or simple to the sublime.

I love looking in boxes of junk at car boot fairs and markets; I love that sense of finding treasure in something someone else has discarded, of finding beauty in something I previously thought ugly.

This piece started with exactly that process, scouring all of my favourite junk haunts looking for discarded hearts. Collecting the hearts, I felt them become a family in my pocket.

Tatty Devine represents who we are, it's about being fun, handmade and original. I try to live every moment of life in a fun way and remember that what makes a beautiful day is not definable in a place, action or thing: you can see beauty if you choose to look at it in a beautiful way.

HARRIET VINE

Make a

TATTY DEVINE
LOVE STORY BRACELET

YOU WILL NEED:

Collection of hearts and vintage trinkets

Beads

Flat-back crystals, googly eyes, foil flowers and cabochons to decorate your charms

Super glue

Spray paint in your favourite colours

Clear acrylic spray coating

Cotton string

Flat and round nose pliers

Jump rings

Chain and clasp

THE MAKE:

1. Wash your hearts and trinkets in lukewarm soapy water to get rid of any dirt, grease and lost love stories. Fresh start. Dry thoroughly with a tea towel. Remove any old metal fastenings with a pair of pliers as you'll be replacing them with shiny new ones.

2. Thread each heart onto thin cotton string and hang, ready for its makeover. It's a good idea to go outside so there's plenty of fresh air when you get the spray paints out.

3. Time to get messy! Choose your favourite colours (we love pretty pastels and bright neons) and spray paint your charms on both sides. Make sure you hang the hearts with plenty of space in between them so the paint doesn't smudge or transfer, then leave to dry for 2–4 hours.

Top Tatty Tip

Explore your local market, jumble sale or charity shop to source a selection of interesting and unusual charms. Look out for shapes with a hole so you can easily attach them to your bracelet or necklace.

4. When dry, give your hearts a coating with clear acrylic spray. This will ensure the paint doesn't peel or come off when you're wearing the bracelet and gives the charms a lovely shiny finish.

5. Lay out all your hearts and choose which ones you'd like to embellish, then use the super glue to attach the decorations to your charms. When finished, let the glue dry overnight.

6. Cut the bracelet chain to your desired length. Attach a clasp to one end of the chain with a jump ring and another jump ring to the other end.

7. We find the best way to add jump rings is to grasp one with a pair of pliers, with the split in the jump ring facing upwards. Take the second pair of pliers in the other hand and, holding them at right angles to the first pair, use them to twist the jump ring apart at the split.

8. Carefully attach your heart to a jump ring and add it to the chain, then use the pliers to firmly pinch it closed. Ta-da!

9. Starting at one end of the chain, continue to firmly pinch and attach your charms to the chain links. Place jump rings in the order you would like them to sit.

Top Tatty Tip

If you're using crystals, make sure you choose ones with a flat back as it's easier to stick them onto your charms.

PETER PILOTTO

We find inspiration and beauty looking at art, architecture and interior design, as well as fashion. When creating we like playing with cinematic perspective, light and shadow, working with classical laces, textiles and technologies, then spinning them together – it's the

unexpected that can end up even more exquisite. Pause from today's high tech and fast pace and look at nature and the natural world surrounding us. Be inspired by the light, the modern and the rainbow-coloured references that are all around – this windmill is like a mini twirling flared skirt: fashion that's child's play.

Make a
PETER PILOTTO
PAPER WINDMILL

YOU WILL NEED:

Template

Thick paper or card

Glue or double-sided sellotape

Stick to mount your windmills on

Penknife or scissors

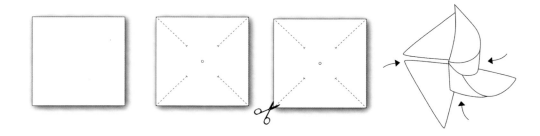

THE MAKE:

1. Take a square of coloured paper or copy the pictures opposite, so you have a different pattern front and back. Mark the cutting lines on one side of the paper.

2. Cut along the lines as shown and bend in the sections to create your windmill twirls.

3. Secure with double-sided sellotape or a spot of glue and fix a stick to the reverse.

4. Instead of a bouquet of flowers, why not fill a vase full of printed paper windmills? Place near a breeze and let the colours blur.

FRONT

BACK

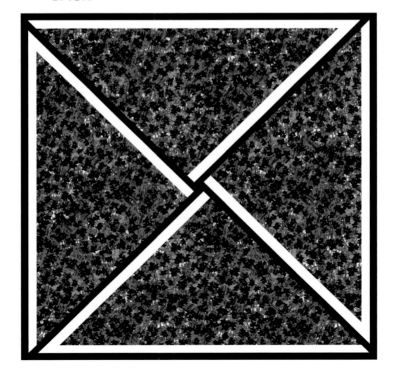

SARA BERMAN

"As a child I inhabited a world very much of my own making; a world inspired by fairytale lands and fantasy characters, where my dolls were my friends, with personalities and peculiarities. In many ways I still exist as that little girl in those fantasy worlds and my love of dolls is still important to me.

As an adult, the visual arts were a natural fit. I engaged first with fashion – a direct response to the transformative power of dress; and latterly to painting, as a way to express myself with a more abstracted freedom. I retain a strong interest in childhood – its naive beauty and simultaneous terror – and the role of nostalgia in memory. Dolls are so emblematic of this for me. I feel it's important to bring aspects of craft to my work – my own methods-based nostalgia if you like. The very act of creating makes me happy – sewing has a rhythm that is both familiar and safe and I find much beauty in that.

The sock puppet princess came about because I wanted to make a doll from something that had already been imbued with a sense of value. I am interested in how a mundane object can be transformed into something else that has huge value. So socks became a princess who needed to be correctly adorned – I chose special buttons from a stash of loved trinkets and each one adds, not only sparkle, but character, emotion and value. Choose carefully; make her beautiful and don't waste the magic.

Beauty and magic are so closely entwined. Beauty is in the eye of the beholder so it is important to behold, to look. As an artist I spend my days looking and this means I see a lot that is beautiful. Beauty sits next to the grotesque, sometimes swapping places as the line is so fine. A beautiful day is one in which the things that I see dance with the things that I make. "

Make a
SARA BERMAN
SCENTED SOCK PRINCESS

YOU WILL NEED:

Pair of cashmere socks

Scissors

Stuffing – ceramic beans, cotton wool or wadding

Lavender

Tulle

Beads, buttons, brocades and trim

Lurex wrist band or scrap piece of wool

THE MAKE:

1. Take one pair of cosy cashmere socks and cut the feet off. The head of the doll will be made from one sock above the ankle to cuff; the body is made from the ankle to cuff of the other sock. The arms and legs are cut lengthways from the toe to heel part of the sock then cut in half: one sock makes two arms, the other sock will make two legs.

2. For the arms and legs: one by one roll your pieces, inside out, longways. Sew down the length to make the 'arms' and 'legs', making sure the 'toe' part is the end part of your tube so you have a neat finish. You can hand-stitch this with a neat little backstitch. Turn right way out again, weigh the bottom of each of the four tubes/limbs with several ceramic beans, then stuff with cotton wool or wadding. Add some lavender to the stuffing if you want Dolly to add a sweet aroma to your room and help ward off moths and uninvited guests.

3. Next you need to make the body to anchor everything to. The body will already be in a tube, as this is the part of the sock that goes from heel to ankle. Turn inside out and sew the raw cut end together, turn right way out and stuff with soft wadding or cotton wool and lavender then sew the ribbed cuff together and even her out.

4. Slice small holes at the sides of the top of the body to insert the top of the arms and sew firmly into place so nothing frays. Add the legs to the bottom edge of the body cuff.

5. The lady now needs her head. Turn your other sock tube inside out and sew around this to create a round curve to seal up the top of the head. Turn right way then stuff, making sure the rib is at the bottom to make her neck.

6. Use a running stitch to gather the neck and attach the head piece to the body. Sew this firmly in place.

7. Now it's time to add the fun things to adorn Dolly. Take a scrap of tulle and wrap this round like a mini skirt, decorating it with buttons, beads or brocade. Source brightly coloured or vintage diamante buttons and give her some style and personality – perhaps chop up a lurex wrist band and use it as a collar for her neck, or add some sparkle to her hair by embroidering pearl beads onto the other half of your wrist band.

8. Eyes are windows to the soul, so don't forget to find her a good pair of buttons – this lady has special vintage Sara Berman peepers. Embroider a smile, or a pout, to suit. Dolly's ready to take her place on the sofa, bed, or anywhere suitably front row.

ALICE MARY LYNCH

"I grew up with two artist parents. I remember sitting in my mum's studio at the top of our old, creaky house, quietly playing with dolls while she painted with oils. I remember the strong smell of turpentine and how she always had paint on her hands. So working in my own world as an artist of sorts did seem the natural way to go. I once wanted to be an actress but now it's my dolls that do all the performing! I like the theatricality of fashion, the combination of creativity and wearability, the stories you can tell and the way clothes come to life when they're worn.

I worked for John Galliano, which was the most inspiring, funny and mad fashion adventure. I was working as a *stagiare* (apprentice) and every day was different, every project was different. We were free to come up with new ideas, we laughed a lot, everything was so flamboyant and theatrical at that time – it was exactly what I thought fashion should be.

We live in such a fast-paced, throwaway society that I love the contradiction of indulging in a longer process, which people have been working with for centuries. It's delicate and beautiful. I find the process of hand-sewing very therapeutic and these little characters encapsulate everything I love to create.

The dancing shadow puppets started with a doodle that seemed to have a little personality which needed to come to life. I have always loved what lies behind the curtain and shadow puppets are just that: a simple way of bringing something to life. I also love the shadows – I find them dreamy, mysterious, romantic. I remember making shadows with our hands in the tent when I camped as a child. It's such a simple way to begin storytelling... I can imagine two cats dancing through the woods together – maybe they'd know how to waltz? The moon would be out and they'd be happy … oh, for a bit of romance!

Take yourself away from the humdrum of your daily life and all the possessions that you probably don't need. Watch the sunset without Instagramming it. Absorb it, just for yourself. Or sit down and make something, not for work, just for pleasure. Start simple and small, listen to your favourite music and enjoy your own space as you sew/stick/draw/paint/dream . . ."

Make

ALICE MARY LYNCH
SHADOW PUPPETS

YOU WILL NEED:

2 A4 pieces of white card

Scissors

Cutting knife

Cutting mat

2 A4 pieces of black card

White pencil

2 small wooden sticks

Sellotape

Anglepoise lamp

Thin white paper or white bed sheet

THE MAKE:

1. Create a 'dancing cat' template on white card and cut it out.

2. Place your template face down on to the black card and draw round it with a white pencil, colouring in the areas to be cut out.

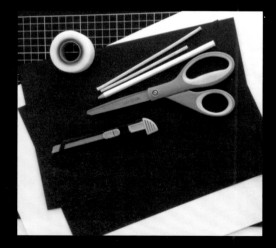

3. Cut your puppet out and fix a stick to the back with sellotape, *et voila*! The cats are now almost ready to dance …

4. Place thin white paper or a sheet over the edge of a table or in a doorway. This will be your screen so choose somewhere suitably dramatic.

5. Cut stars, a crescent moon, or other shapes out of the remaining black card and tape them to the back of the screen.

6 . Position your lamp behind the sheet and light it up.

7. Hold the cats behind the screen and let your story begin …whether you're telling a fairytale or sharing the latest gossip, they'll bring some poetry to bedtime.

JO LOVES

As soon as I wake up the first scent that hits me is a combination of Pomelo-scented bed sheets and strong builder's tea. It's a good example of my approach to fragrance: blending an unexpected mix of smells and ingredients together to create something new and extraordinary.

For me, scent is my means of communication and I surround myself with it wherever I am. I live in a completely white house and use fragrance to transform each room… you could say I paint with fragrance! The smells you run through your home are extremely personal and there are no rules, but I think citrus scents freshen up an entrance hall or living room and calming florals in bedrooms and bathrooms work well, as they help calm and relax. Candlelight instantly transforms the mood and feeling of a room and I love to fill the whole house with candles, especially as it gets dark – it's absolutely magical!

My work is a reflection of me and so I pour all of the things I love into fragrance: memories, moments, music and colour. Everything I do has to have integrity. I started my career mixing face creams in my kitchen using just four plastic jugs and a saucepan and so I love anything that allows me to chop, blend, mix or melt to 'make' something new. The scented hearts were created because I wanted to scent my wardrobe and drawers with a fine fragrance and not an air freshener or drawer liners. They are so simple and quick to make. I've also given them to my girlfriends in linen bags ready to hang up.

Find just five minutes every day to enjoy something that inspires you. Often inspiration is the oxygen that allows innovation and creativity to breathe. To feel inspired you have to find something that makes your heart beat. Feeling happy and fulfilled makes life beautiful.   JO MALONE

Make

JO LOVES
SCENTED HEARTS

YOU WILL NEED:

Scented candle wax (remnants of a burned candle)

Saucepan, preferably with a lip for pouring

Wooden spoon

Essential oil (lemongrass, lavender, basil, mint)

Heart-shaped moulds (an ice-cube tray in heart shapes is perfect)

Small linen or muslin bag(s)

Ribbon

THE MAKE:

1. Ensuring that all the wicks have been removed, carefully take the last remnants of wax from your favourite scented candles and place them in a saucepan over a low heat.

2. Once they are fully melted, remove from the heat and stir in five drops of your chosen essential oil. Try different oils depending on which room you want to scent.

3. Leave to cool and gently pour into your heart-shaped moulds. Leave to set.

4. Once hard, pop out your scented wax hearts and place a few in the linen bag(s). Tie with ribbon and hang in your favourite room or closet.

CATH KIDSTON

I love mixing prints and colours, and vintage
and modern. I guess it all stems from *Blue Peter*!
I do love making things, in particular with other people.
We had a huge jam-making session this summer with
all ages helping. The jam wasn't very good but it was so
much fun!

When I started my business, most of my stock was
vintage but I soon started making my own cheerful,
practical home stuff – floral ironing-board covers and
suchlike, and it went from there. I wanted to make fun,
affordable things for me and my friends. Whether it's an
item of clothing or an interiors piece, it has to have a
good energy. Homes are always best when they reflect
their owners. There needs to be a sense of warmth and
surprise.

The best way to make life beautiful? Humour.
It's a cliché but laughter is the best beauty tonic on the
market. I hope this felt tea brings a smile to your
face!

Make a

CATH KIDSTON
HIGH (FELT) TEA

YOU WILL NEED:

Felt in cake and sandwich colours

Thread in colours to match the felt

Needle

Wadding

Fabric glue

Fabric scissors

Yellow scourer sponges

THE MAKE:

WHITE BREAD SANDWICH

1. Place one long brown strip of felt along the L-shape of one cream triangle and stitch the edges together where the two pieces meet. Take a second cream triangle and repeat along the other edge of another brown strip. Stuff the inside gap with wadding, then use a short cream strip to close the gap, stitching along all edges. Repeat to make your second sliced bread triangle.

2. Arrange your felt fillings of choice (cheese, cucumber, lettuce, ham and tomato perhaps?) on top of one bread half, just as you would a real sandwich, using fabric glue to stick each piece down as you go on. Top with the second bread half and glue into place.

JAMMY DODGER BISCUIT

1. For the top biscuit, with its famous jammy hole, cut 2 cream felt rings, sew around the inner circle and outer edge and fill with wadding.

2. For the base biscuit: place a piece of wadding between two cream full circles and stitch around the edge.

3. Your filling will consist of one full white 'cream' circle and one red 'jam' felt circle. Layer the white and red circle in between the two biscuits, gluing them together as you go.

For this high tea all delicacies are sewn together using a blanket stitch. Each instruction makes one cake but, as with real cake, you might want more than one slice!

VICTORIA SPONGE

1. Starting from the bottom, layer together one sponge wedge, three white (cream) felt triangles, one red (jam) triangle and a second sponge wedge, gluing each layer in place as you go. Then glue your large white felt icing piece to wrap over the end and cover the top of the cake layers.

2. Stitch together two red cherry circles, padded with some wadding, and sew into place on the top of the iced cake slice.

FONDANT FANCY

1. Take a long rectangular piece of felt and stitch it so it attaches around the edges to a felt square in a matching colour. Sew on a second square to create its 'lid', leaving one edge open to stuff with wadding. Add an additional small ball of wadding (about the size of a 10p coin) under the middle of the top square to create the raised icing bump, then sew the final edge closed.

2. To decorate, cut very thin strips of contrasting coloured felt, and glue to the top square.

BATTENBERG CAKE

1. Stitch two small yellow felt squares onto opposite corners of one large pink square to create the Battenberg's signature checkerboard effect. Repeat for the second side of the cake slice.

2. Take a long thin cream piece of felt and stitch it along the edges of one large square. Sew on the second square, leaving one side open, stuff with wadding, then sew the final edge closed.

ANYA HINDMARCH

" You can find inspiration everywhere and anywhere, in anything and everything – from people to architecture, travel to chocolate.

I was fifteen when my mother gave me her old Gucci handbag. I think this started my love of accessories and obsession with craftsmanship. I believe that luxury always involves sentiment and humour as well as craftsmanship, and

fashion should make you smile! Women play so many different roles in life – I am a mother, wife and businesswoman and I also like to have fun – so I design with all these roles in mind. I think bags can really make a difference to how a woman feels and the 'role' she plays.

To make life beautiful, remember that things come of things! If you drop a pebble in a puddle of water you get ripples. If you throw energy at things you get energy back. "

ANYA HINDMARCH
BOW PRETZELS

YOU WILL NEED:

FOR THE DOUGH

1kg plain white flour, plus extra for dusting

2 tsp fast-action dried yeast

260ml lukewarm water

260ml lukewarm milk

2 tbsp salt

80g unsalted butter, melted

1 tbsp malt extract

3 tbsp bicarbonate of soda

Sea salt

Makes 14 pretzels

THE MAKE:

1. Mix 100g of the flour with the yeast and lukewarm water in a bowl. Cover with cling film and leave to rise in a warm place for at least 5 hours.

Add flour, yeast and water

2. Tie on your best pinny, take off any jewels and roll up your sleeves. Add the remaining flour, milk, salt, melted butter and malt extract then knead until firm (this workout takes around 10 minutes).

3. Cover and leave the bowl again in that warm place for another 1½ hours, or until the dough springs back when pushed gently.

4. Place dough on a work surface lightly dusted with flour and roll a handful into a 40cm-long rope (if this seems too big, modify accordingly).

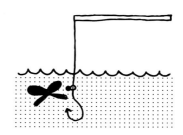

5. Fold one end (A) and loop it across the middle section as shown in the diagram. Repeat with the other side, folding end B across the middle section. Twist end B around the intersection and – tah-dah! – a finished bow.

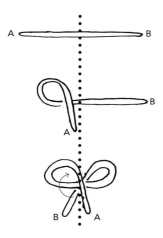

6. Repeat until you have twisted all your dough into bows and leave uncovered on baking trays in a warm place for 30 minutes to settle into their shape.

7. Once the dough has risen, place the trays somewhere cool. This helps to develop a 'skin' on the pretzels, which gives them their chewy texture.

8. Pre-heat the oven to 200°C/gas mark 6 and bring 1.5 litres of water to the boil in a large saucepan and add the bicarbonate of soda. Be safe – wear rubber gloves and goggles for this bit.

9. One by one, place dough bows into the boiling liquid until they float to the surface. Carefully fish them out with a slotted spoon, or chosen kitchen 'hook' implement, and place on a baking tray lined with non-stick baking paper.

10. Sprinkle your bows with sea salt and make 1cm deep cuts at the thickest part of the bow. Place tray in the pre-heated oven and cook for around 15 minutes until the pretzels have turned dark brown, then remove from the oven and transfer to a wire rack to cool.

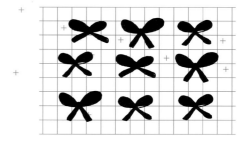

11. If you think your handiwork too pretty to eat, loop tinsel through them and hang from a Christmas tree, or make smaller versions, glue a safety pin on the back and wear as a brooch.

ANTHROPOLOGIE

" Art and creativity are the very DNA of Anthropologie. Our buyers and designers travel the world to discover unusual products and to collaborate with talented artists.

We believe in doing things differently; it's individuality that makes life beautiful. So why not create your own paper placemats using a montage of mugs as your inspiration? "

Make

ANTHROPOLOGIE
PERSONALISED PLACEMATS

YOU WILL NEED:

Alphabet templates

Scissors

Sellotape and glue

Paper

Colouring pens and glitter

THE MAKE:

1. Photocopy or scan then print a selection of the tea cups opposite.

2. Cut out the cups to create the names of your guests, glue on glitter, add your own colours and fix them to a plain piece of paper

3. Places please! Dinner is served.

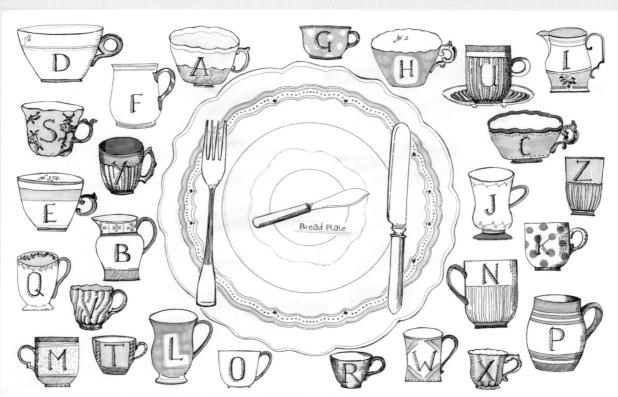

LULU GUINNESS

"I was born looking for something different. I was always drawing and sketching – I was terrified of being bored. I always liked things very camp. I liked musicals, movie stars; I was intrigued by the writer Gertrude Lawrence, the collector Peggy Guggenheim and the designer Elsa Schiaparelli.

When I had my first child I decided I wanted to work from home, so I set myself up in our basement and eventually designed a woman's briefcase called the 'Lulu bag'. Luckily for me, it ended up selling fantastically well! I was thrilled to have found the perfect outlet for my creativity, so continued to design more bags – and the rest, as they say, is history.

When it comes to dinner parties, I prefer attending to hosting. But if I am entertaining, then I only have one rule: there are no rules. Then it's bound to go with a bang! My fantasy guests would include my classic heroes – Beaton, Schiaparelli, Hitchcock, Blumenfeld, Steinberg – and Thomas Heatherwick is a genius, he'd be a great contemporary addition.

The idea behind this project is a bit of a play on the title of a great film starring Sidney Poitier, *Guess Who's Coming to Dinner* – watch it! Make the seats up as blondes, redheads and brunettes – as a brunette I don't think it's blondes that have the most fun!"

LULU GUINNESS
DINNER PARTY CHAIR COVERS

YOU WILL NEED:

White pillowcases (2 or 4: don't dine alone with this idea)

Coloured felt (use finished ladies as your muse)

Sewing machine

Black, red and burgundy cotton thread (or other colours according to the felts and character chosen)

Needle

Fabric glue (optional)

Tracing paper

Scissors

Chalk or marker pen

Pins

Iron

THE MAKE:

1. Select your lady/guest and create a template, using either your imagination or one of Lulu's two designs as your starting inspiration.

2. Chalk around the templates onto your felt and cut out the pieces.

3. Unpick the sides of the pillowcase (this makes it easier to sew on the features).

4. Iron the pillowcase so that you have a flat surface to fashion her up on.

5. Pin the felt shapes to the pillowcase then carefully sew them on using a straight stitch on your sewing machine. Start with the hair and straight lines – or, if you prefer, use a fabric glue instead.

6. Turn the pillowcase inside out and sew the seams back down.

7. Turn her right way out and place on the back of a chair. Now create a party – fashion a pillowcase for each guest.

173

JULIEN MACDONALD

"I have always loved fashion. Whilst at art college in Wales we would have weekly life drawing classes but I could never draw the nude figure simply as it was. I couldn't help draping them in amazing fabric and textiles: it was then I realised that I wanted to be a designer.

Every woman has a little black dress in their wardrobe; it has become a staple garment and an absolute essential. The LBD can take you from day to night effortlessly, especially as they are so easy to dress up with amazing jewellery! As people are so busy these days it makes looking fabulous all the time much easier. I have always been inspired by old Hollywood actresses and my favourite aesthetic, glamorous chic, is a nod to Marilyn Monroe and Audrey Hepburn. My LBD style is very flattering and accentuates the best parts of a woman's body. The trimmings on this LBD are a combination of antique lace and trimmings bought from local haberdasheries. You don't have to be a fashion expert to pull this off – just find some gorgeous old vintage lace in tonal shades of black and explore your local haberdasheries for elements to decorate this with.

The trick is always to wear something you feel comfortable in, because if you feel confident on the inside you will look more beautiful on the outside. Don't try to be overly fashionable – it's better to wear something you feel truly great in."

Make a

JULIEN MACDONALD
LITTLE BLACK DRESS

YOU WILL NEED:

Floral lace, motifs, sequins, crystals, beads, embroidery trim, black tulle (gather a selection)

Little black dress

Black grosgrain ribbon (approx. 80cm)

Dressmaker's pins

Black thread

Needle

Sharp scissors

Your creativity!

THE MAKE:

1. Lay out trims, embroideries and sewing tools on a clear flat surface. Select your favourite pieces and play around with pinning them to your dress.

2. Choose a piece of black floral lace and carefully cut out flower clusters in varying sizes. Trim off any excess lace so the flowers are perfectly pruned. Once you have enough flowers to embellish the neckline, play around with symmetry and positioning before pinning them on. When you're happy, stitch into place.

3. For an extra finishing touch, take two larger floral motifs and place on either side by your collar bone to make the shoulders 'pop' and give the dress a trendy edge. Sew these in place.

ribbon. If your focal point has been created separately you'll now need to sew the ribbon to the back of the embroidered piece, making sure there's an equal excess (approx. 40cm) of ribbon on each side. Trim the ends of the ribbon and tie in a generous bow.

5. Your little black dress is now ready for a night on the town! Style with a pair of brightly coloured or printed heels with matching clutch to set off the look. Go out and find the most glamorous party in town – you look fabulous!

4. Now make a belt to accentuate your curves and cinch your waist. To do this, take a long length of black grosgrain ribbon. In the centre, create a focal point either by fashioning a piece of embroidery or by sewing beads and crystals to the

THEODORA & CALLUM

"We have known each other for over fifteen years and were friends long before we started our label Theodora & Callum. In many ways we're total opposites, both in the way we dress and the way we think, but we both wanted to create something that women could return to year after year and that made them feel glamorous and adventurous. Scarves are a wonderful way to do this as they can be draped and tied and knotted in so many different ways. Here's how to turn our scarf into a necklace!"

THEODORA & CALLUM
STATEMENT NECKLACE

THE MAKE:

1. Cut your scarf into 1.5m long and 4cm wide strips.

2. Attach one jump ring to each end of the gold chain then connect the clasp to one of the rings.

3. Pull one strip of the scarf through the jump ring on the end of the chain until the scarf hangs evenly on each side.

4. Gently begin to braid the chain with the scarf strips.

5. When you've finished braiding, take the remaining ends of the scarf strips and pull them through the last hole of the chain. Glue the excess scarf around the braided ends to secure and style as your mood takes you.

YOU WILL NEED:

1 Theodora & Callum scarf (or silk/thin cotton scarf)

Scissors

2 large jump rings

Approx. 75cm gold-coloured chain

1 medium-sized gold clasp

Fabric or strong all-purpose glue

HOLLY FULTON'S PAPER JEWELLERY

HOLLY FULTON

"I first started to think about fashion consciously aged twelve when preparing for my first school disco. I decided to wear a half-black, half-white ensemble, which was the source of vigorous comment from the rest of the party and the start of a chequered (literally) relationship with fashion. For me, impact has always been the key factor. I've always been drawn to pattern and colour and to express this through clothing seems natural.

I grew up surrounded by books and objects and my parents were captivated by early twentieth-century design. Particularly strong presences were Art Deco and Jessie M. King, whose intense rendered style of drawing has come through in my own. Eduardo Paolozzi is a huge influence on me. I look at his work and think it looks like the inside of my head: an explosive mix of pop and pattern.

Life is beautiful for many reasons. Most important are the people you surround yourself with. That and the glory of the Scottish countryside. I'm a sucker for the motherland. I find inspiration everywhere – that's what's fun about being a designer. I am a natural hoarder and gravitate to car boot sales for visual stimulation. Genuine inspiration can often be found in the simplest and most unexpected places.

I'm in the privileged position of having my own label, and every item I realise as part of that is a joy. I hope people feel inspired as they make this paper jewellery and exude confidence when they wear it. I like to imagine it being worn in unexpected situations – when getting a pint of milk, walking the dog – as much as in more glamorous locations. Fashion is a tool to represent yourself and your personality.

To make your own life beautiful, lose negativity and embrace life, no matter what it brings. Everything will seem so much better once you learn to expect the unexpected and grab any opportunity with both hands. And try to do all the above in as colourful and heavily accessorised a way as possible!"

HOLLY FULTON
PAPER JEWELLERY

YOU WILL NEED:

Good-quality plain paper

Photocopier

Scissors

Mount board or card

Needle

Jump rings

Choker, chain, earring attachments

THE MAKE:

1. Find your favourite elements in the illustration (see p. 182 for the template) and copy them onto good-quality paper, then stick onto mount board or card.

2. Cut out the design – in pieces if necessary.

3. Once you've decided how you'd like to piece the elements together, pierce holes in the card and join together using the jump rings. Attach your design to a choker, chain or studs.

4. Find a fashionable location and wow people with your inventiveness.

JASPER CONRAN

"The first thing that I can remember making was a shiny plastic raincoat for my Action Man – very wet look, very fabulous. Unfortunately the scissors slipped and I cut myself badly so I ended up in A&E. I still have the scar.

I can't really pinpoint where my ideas come from. It could be from a book or a film or a painting or anything really. I see things and file them in my memory and then they pop up at unexpected times and help to inspire me.

Quite often it can be a mixture of unrelated influences that converge. I can't really say why I chose to make a lobster cushion, the idea just crawled into my head and amused me. I do think that the secret of taste is to throw the whole idea out of the window every now and then and indulge in the not-so-SERIOUS… Being creative is a gift which, if used well, has the power to make people happy, which is not to be sniffed at!!"

JASPER CONRAN
LOBSTER CUSHION

YOU WILL NEED:

Lobster template

Pencil

Scissors

Orange felt

Black felt, enough to cover cushion,
2 x 32 x 42cm pieces

Tacking thread

Embroidery needles

Contrasting colour embroidery threads

Chalk

2 beads (for eyes)

30 x 40cm cushion pad

THE MAKE:

1. Create a lobster template, draw round it on orange felt and cut out the pieces.

2. Position all parts of the lobster in orange felt onto the black felt then tack into place.

3. Blanket stitch all the way around the edge of each lobster piece in a contrasting coloured thread.

4. Add antennae: copy the design shown or practise on tracing paper then mark your outline lightly in white chalk on the black felt before you chain stitch over this. Don't forget to sew on two beads, one for each eye.

5. Finally, blanket stitch two sides of the two black felt pieces together. Place the cushion pad inside and stitch the remaining two sides closed, covering the cushion pad. Your lobster is ready. Serve on your sofa, solo or with like-minded crustacean cushions.

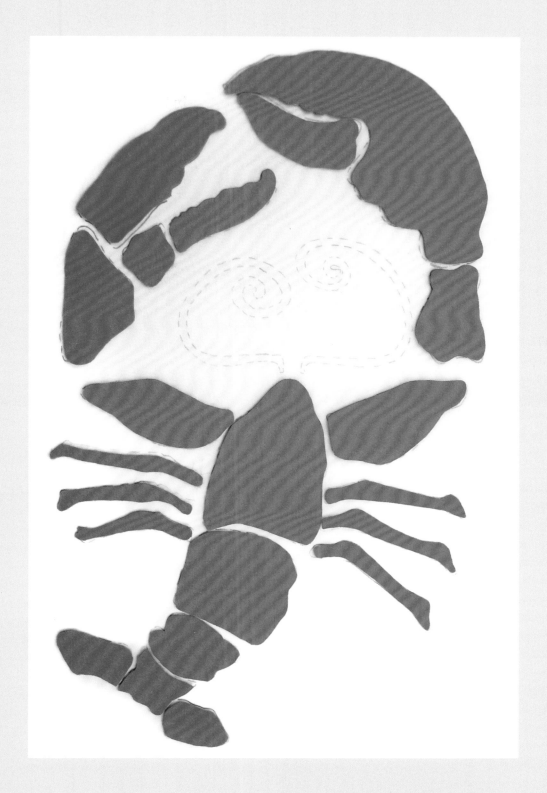

189

PIERS ATKINSON

" Friends, family and peace are what make life beautiful – they are also a good place to look for inspiration. Inspiration is in everything, but a slight sense of rebellious humour or mild 'naughtiness' can give the best results.

I fell into millinery by (happy!) accident. I was working in fashion, wearing many proverbial hats – PR, editorial publishing, working for the iconic Zandra Rhodes and at Fashion Week. In the middle of all this I made a small collection of nine pieces just to see what reaction they would get … it went into *Vogue* and ended up on the front row at Prada, so all my other 'hats' went on hold.

I grew up in Norfolk with three generations of women – my mother, the theatrical milliner Hilary Elliott; my sister

Lucy, the long-suffering photographic model for teenage reconstructions of Grace Jones and Art of Noise record covers; and my grandmother, the artist, writer, horticulturalist and illustrator Lesley Gordon, from whom I took my multi-disciplinary cue. From the very beginning, I created hats purely for the fun of it. It all started under the kitchen table using off-cuts from Mum's incredible pieces for the opera houses – and then, like magic, a hobby became a career.

This accidental start taught me to be fearless – no idea or experiment should ever be disregarded. Women have incredible nerve and style, and the pieces I thought might be too outrageous are the ones that sell the best. I've learned a lot about business and even more about people through millinery!' "

Make a
PIERS ATKINSON
HIGH-HEELED GEISHA HEADBAND

YOU WILL NEED:

Faux silk flowers

Glitter or clear glitter nail varnish

Super glue

Fabric-covered headband

Small paintbrush

Barbie shoes (as many as she'll give you)

Bradawl (or ad lib with a kilt pin or needle)

Scissors

Needle

Fishing thread, yarn or strong invisible thread

Bugle beads

Sellotape / masking tape

THE MAKE:

1. Decorate silk flowers with glitter either by dotting super glue around the edges of the petals and sprinkling glitter over them or by rolling the petals in a saucer of glitter. Alternatively, add sparkle using clear glitter nail varnish.

2. Pin or glue the silk flowers to the headband styled in your chosen position. The headband should be 'invisible' so choose one as thin as possible and ideally matched to your hair colour.

3. Carefully pierce a hole in the ankle of each of Barbie's heels using a bradawl, kilt pin or needle.

4. Cut a 15cm length of thread and start to feed the shoes and bugle beads onto the thread to create your 'Fashion Geisha Waterfall' effect. Make up three to five strands depending on how many shoes Barbie can spare.

5. Hold the threads in position on your headband and put it up to your face to check how they fall. Adjust until fabulous, using masking tape to hold them at the correct angle while you get your needle ready.

6. Sew each high-heeled thread onto the headband and ensure they are secure. You are ready for an enchanted evening.

AMANDA HARLECH

"There is someone in the garden –
always watching from the turn in the
park, where the foliage thickens; an eye
or a blackberry or a bird or Pan – or my
scarecrow who moves in the dark. I see the
grass flattened beneath the apple tree . . .
maybe she rested there beneath the owl swoop
while a fox worked his way homeward at dawn.
My scarecrow lives in a world of green. She
is an all-weather guardian of the vegetable
patch and the orchard. With a cruciform made
from two broom sticks held with baking
twine, I tied in a skirt of reeds, binding her at
the waist.

I dress her for each season or equinox or
lady day – overalls and old jackets and a
balaclava for the snow, old tablecloths and
sheets with a straw hat and a veil for the sun.
In their most intimidating form scarecrows
are nearly human; wicker men, dervish
dancing girls, versions of yourself in the
garden."

Make an

AMANDA HARLECH SCARECROW

YOU WILL NEED:

Garden

Broomstick

2 wire coat hangers

Thatching reeds, from gardening centre or roof thatcher

Chicken wire

Lots of baking twine or tough string

Fancy dress mask or a pair of pale tights

Old clothes, gloves, socks, as much as you can fashion up

Paper

Emulsion/oil-based paint

THE MAKE:

1. Take the broomstick (or sturdy 2m stick or bamboo cane) to create the core frame and then use wire coat hangers to form the shoulder structure of your silhouette. Use one hanger per shoulder, bending the frame so half of the hanger lies on the broomstick – the other forms the shoulder, which you should then bend into the top half of the arm.

2. Now, either drape an old shirt over this structure, with shirt arms over the 'shoulders', then stuff with reeds or chicken wire scrunched and tied into place; or take baking twine and tie bundles of reeds over the hanger and broomstick frame to fill the silhouette. You can extend the reeds down the body and create a skirt of reeds, or dress the scarecrow in something seasonal, just don't forget gloves for hands and old wellingtons or marrows for feet! Use your twine and wrap around arms and waist to shape as much as hold stuffing in place. Style is essential – especially if all eyes are going to be on you.

3. Don't forget her head! From the shoulders twist chicken wire onto the hangers / into the shoulder line and up to hold the 'head' – which can be a fancy dress mask, papier mâché or, for a softer alternative, stuff the leg of a pair of pale tights with old socks, hay and paper and mould into a head shape. Paint on features with emulsion or oil-based paint so her features don't run. Add a hat, an old wig or ringlets of cassette tapes or old tea towels or ribbons. Be sure she has character that is as forbidding as Miss Haversham.

4. Once the essential underpinning is in place, it's time to place her in position and get ready to dress her up.

ALL-WEATHER SCARECROW STYLE TIPS

Dress your lady for the season, the equinox or Lady Day. Paint the face as many times as you want – change her character, change her look. A scarecrow doesn't mind so long as he or she is given a heart!

Wind and Wet

Layer black bin liners and plastic bags and tie them together in a patchwork pattern. Give your scarecrow a turban, a necklace of CDs and sunglasses and style ringlets out of old cassette tapes.

Snow

The snow magnifies the shape of the scarecrow so add lots of layers – old ski jackets, balaclavas, hats, and socks as mittens or old sportswear cut into scarves, with baking twine to cinch it all in. If she looks lonely out in the cold, build snowmen in a circle to keep your scarecrow company.

Sun

Use old sheets and tablecloths for sunny days and style with straw hat and net curtains, like a Victorian bee-keeper beautifully veiled. Add flowers or ribbons and why not find a birdcage for her to hold – just in case the greedy pigeons weren't getting the message!

MICHAEL HOWELLS
AND
CHRISTIAN LACROIX

"I must have been about eleven when I watched [production designer] Eileen Diss on *Blue Peter.* She had designed a production of *The Count of Monte Cristo* and was explaining her designs and model machetes. I think it was as she explained how it went from idea to model to thing that I realised, 'Oh-my-goodness, I want to do that!' And that was it.

Theatre is a portal for the imagination – it is there to inspire, to make you laugh, to make you weep… It can transport you to a new world that's within your reach – so you need to pick up the scissors, turn off the internet and turn on your imagination. This is a set with no script, with fantastic figurines by Christian Lacroix. Let ideas ricochet and the performance begin…

All the world's a stage… and here is yours… " MICHAEL HOWELLS

Make a
MICHAEL HOWELLS AND CHRISTIAN LACROIX THEATRE OF FASHION

YOU WILL NEED:

Theatre template

Card

Scalpel or scissors

Glue

Lollipop sticks

THE MAKE:

1. Copy the theatre (see templates starting on p. 208) onto card, cut and fold.

2. Choose your scene, characters and stage entrances and exits.

3. Attach a lollipop stick, or length of card, to Christian Lacroix's cast.

4. Give the performance of your life.

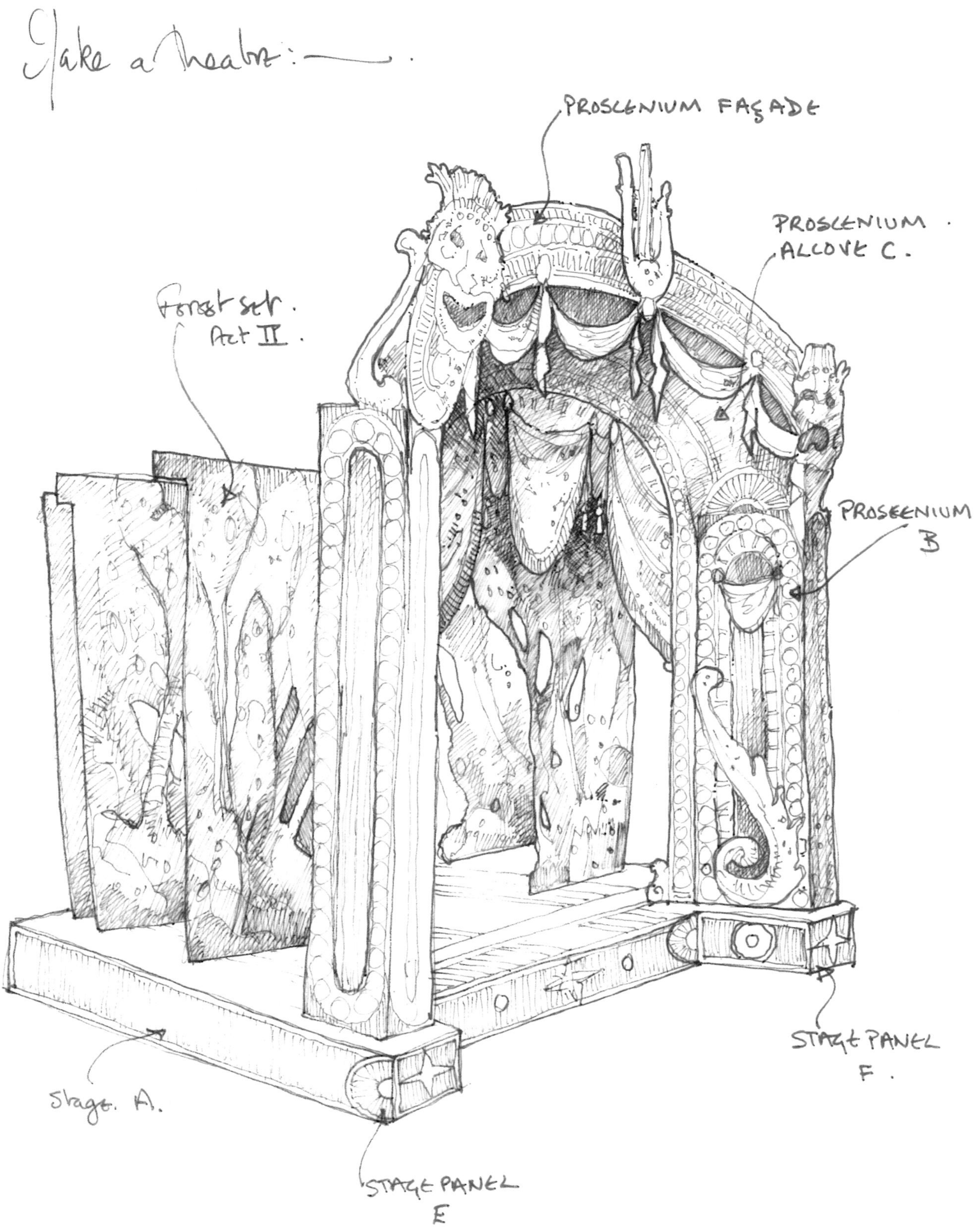

Make a Theatre:—

PROSCENIUM FAÇADE

PROSCENIUM
ALCOVE C.

Forest set.
Act II.

PROSCENIUM
B

PROSCENIUM
B

Stage. A.

STAGE PANEL
F.

STAGE PANEL
E

TEMPLATES

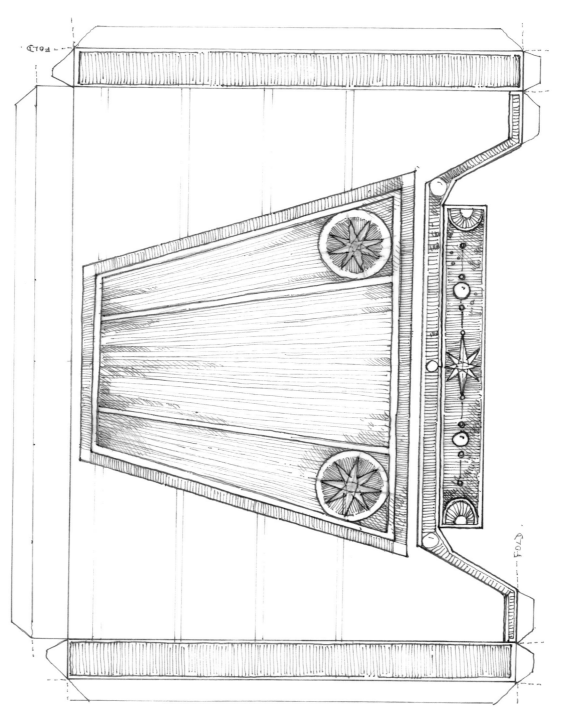

FLOOR A.

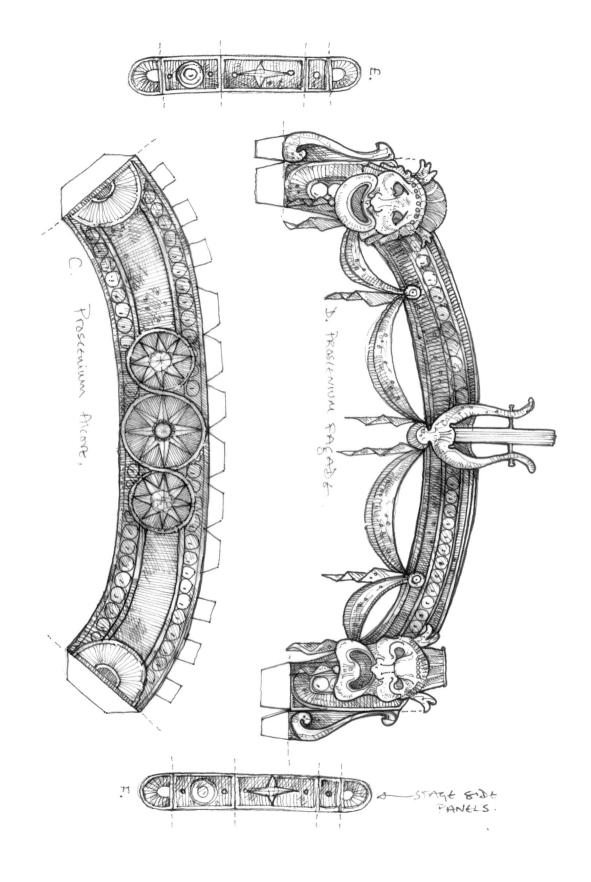

C. Proscenium Arcave.

D. Proscenium Façade

STAGE SIDE PANELS.

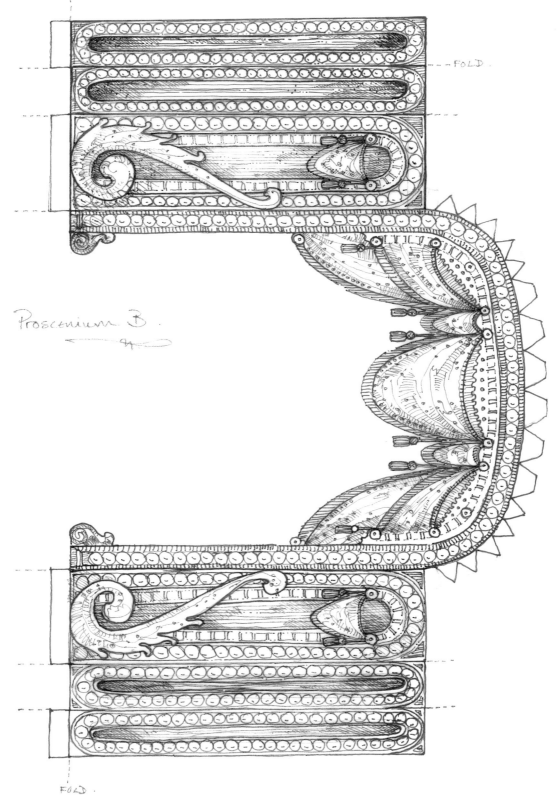

Proscenium B.

FOLD

FOLD

211

Forest Backcloth.

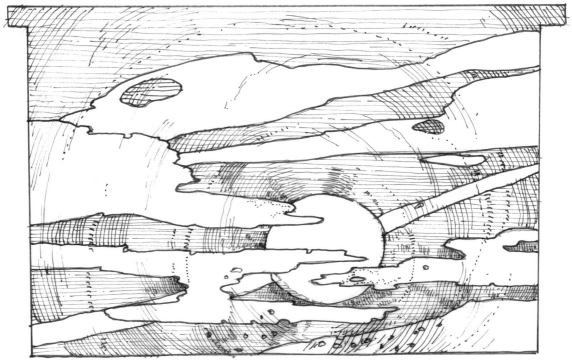

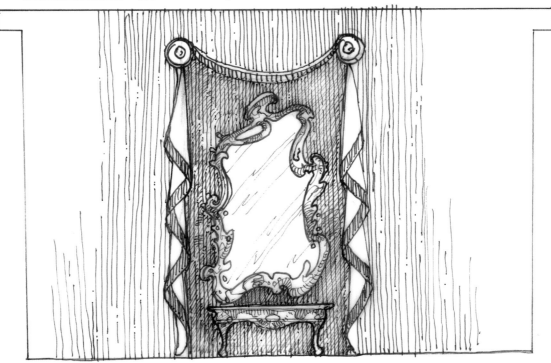

Ballroom Back Cloth.

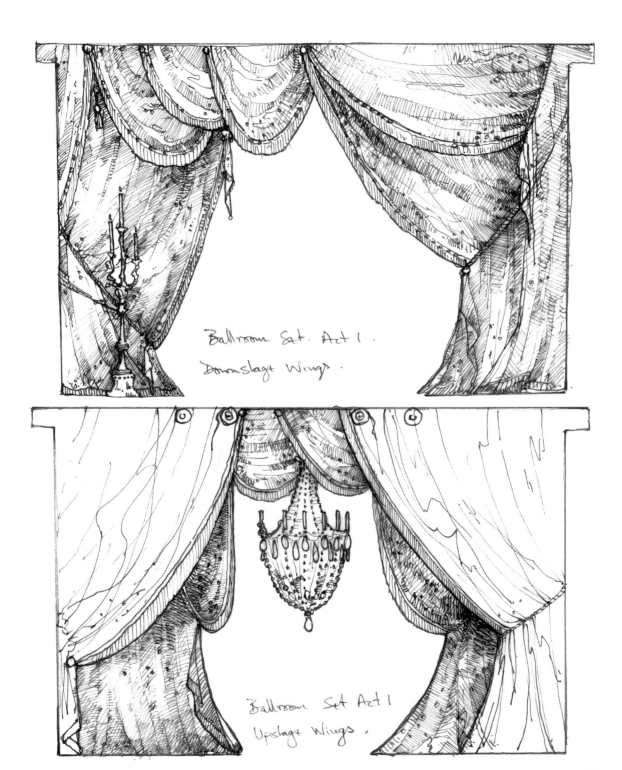

Ballroom Set. Act 1.
Downstage Wings.

Ballroom Set Act 1
Upstage Wings.

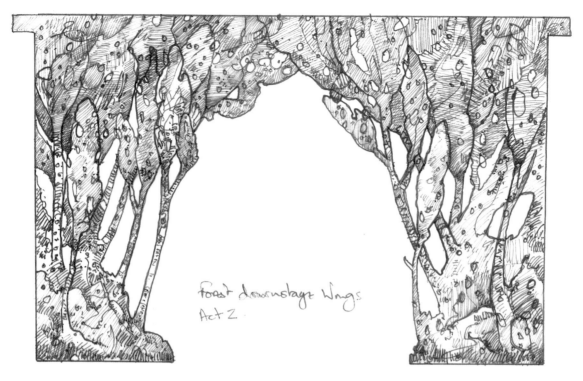

Forest downstage Wings
Act 2.

Forest
Upstage Wings
Act 2.

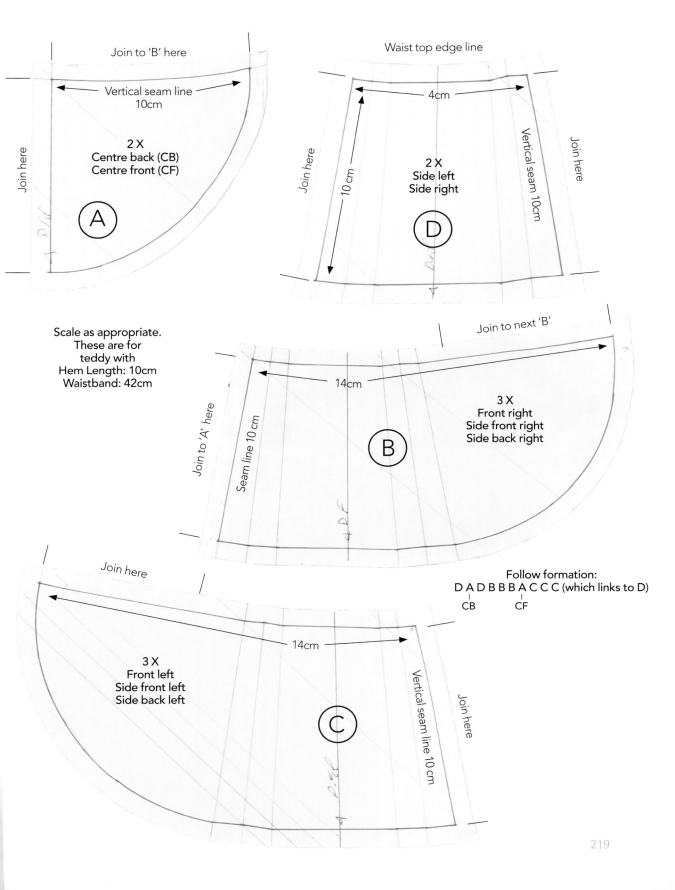

Join to 'B' here

← Vertical seam line →
10cm

Join here

2 X
Centre back (CB)
Centre front (CF)

A

Waist top edge line

← 4cm →

Join here

↕ 10 cm

2 X
Side left
Side right

Vertical seam 10cm

Join here

D

Scale as appropriate.
These are for
teddy with
Hem Length: 10cm
Waistband: 42cm

Join to next 'B'

← 14cm →

Join to 'A' here

Seam line 10 cm

3 X
Front right
Side front right
Side back right

B

Join here

← 14cm →

3 X
Front left
Side front left
Side back left

Vertical seam line 10 cm

Join here

C

Follow formation:
D A D B B B A C C C (which links to D)
    | |
   CB   CF

219

BIOGRAPHIES

Alice Mary Lynch spent nine years in Paris working in couture ateliers, embroidering and embellishing beautiful gowns, before moving home to Somerset where she is now a doll-maker. Each whimsical doll is fashioned with beads, tulles and the same attention to detail she applied in the Parisian salons, and clients include Alice Temperley, Victoria Beckham and Anya Hindmarch.
www.alicemarylynch.com

Amanda Harlech is one of the most creative and inspiring women in fashion. She was a fashion editor at *Harpers and Queen* when she met and began working with John Galliano on the narrative of his first collections. In 1996 she joined Karl Lagerfeld at Chanel to become one of his collaborators and creative confidantes. Amanda styles, inspires, writes stories, consults on Fendi and, when at home in Shropshire, rides horses.
instagram.com/amandaharlech

Anthropologie is the American lifestyle and fashion brand that scours the globe to source treasures and trinkets so you don't have to. They collaborate with artists and designers, host DIY workshops, fashion shows and events, and create an eclectic and unique alphabet of inspiration for the home.
www.anthropologie.eu

Anya Hindmarch is the English accessories designer whose namesake label was founded in 1987. From the very first handbag to her runway extravaganzas at London Fashion Week, this is a brand with a sense of humour. Anya's creations are beautifully crafted, always bespoke and often opinionated, and include the 'Be A Bag' and 'I'm Not a Plastic Bag' campaign. Hindmarch is also a director of the British Fashion Council and a UK trade ambassador.
www.anyahindmarch.com

Bella Freud embodies all the cool of her cult London fashion label, founded in 1990. Freud was born in London, daughter of artist Lucien Freud, and studied in Rome before working for Vivienne Westwood and Ossie Clark. From fashion shows staged in nightclubs and film collaborations with John Malkovich to friends and muses that include Anita Pallenberg, Suzie Bick, Kate Moss and Alison Mosshart, Freud creates knitwear with attitude. She is also founder of the Hoping Foundation.
www.bellafreud.com

Benjamin Seidler is both illustrator and jewellery designer, studying fashion at Central St Martins and architecture at Cambridge. He has designed prints for Asprey's silk scarves, written for the *International Herald Tribune* and designed accessories at luxury houses including Acne, Anya Hindmarch, Prada, Miu Miu and Katie Hillier. Seidler is now a full-time designer in New York.
www.benjaminseidler.com

The **British Fashion Council** was founded in 1983 to help promote and celebrate the British fashion industry. The BFC hosts the biannual London Fashion Week, where over 250 designers are showcased and £100 million-worth of orders are generated: fashion is big business. From London Fashion Week (Womens) and London Collections: Mens to the annual British Fashion Awards, the BFC tirelessly showcases and supports emerging and established designers at showrooms worldwide.
www.britishfashioncouncil.co.uk

Cambridge Satchel Company is proudly 'Made in England'. It was founded in 2008 by Julie Deane as a means to an end: she needed to pay school fees, and she couldn't find a traditional school satchel anywhere. Started at her kitchen table, the business soon expanded in shape, size and colour as the fashion and celebrity world all became fans. In 2013 she won a Great British Entrepreneur Award

and the Queen's Award for International Trade and was 'Made In The UK' UK Manufacturer of the Year 2014 – and the company continues to expand and prove you are never too old to carry a satchel.
www.cambridgesatchel.com

Cath Kidston is the English fashion and interiors designer whose popular nostalgia-chic brand is inspired by the colours, prints and fabrics of her childhood home. With vintage-feel fabrics and prints that celebrate souvenirs of London and country flowers, this quintessentially English brand adds yester-year charm with a modern-day twist to the wardrobe and the home.
www.cathkidston.com

Charlotte Olympia takes the glamour of Hollywood and creates luxury shoes and accessories that mix a love of fashion with the coquettish art of corsetry and being a woman. Having trained at Cordwainers, she launched her shoe brand in 2008 and placed sophisticated and sassy shoes on the pedestal (or platform?) they deserve. From kitty-cat flats to towering heels, Charlotte's web believes there's no business like shoe business.
uk.charlotteolympia.com

Chinti and Parker was founded in 2009 by cousins Anna Singh and Rachael Wood. This British label combines comfort with cool, and their no-fuss philosophy is 'clothes you can be yourself in'. Crafted with clever detailing, they produce signature knits and timeless pieces with understated effortless elegance.
www.chintiandparker.com

Christian Lacroix is the legendary French couturier and costumier. He opened his haute couture house in 1987, his ready-to-wear line in 1988, and produced collections that exploded with opulent colour, prints, puff-balls and *joie de vivre*. From crinolines to corsets, storytelling to stationery, he mixes together the hot colours of his Mediterranean hometown in high fashion. He produced the 2013 Schiaparelli haute couture tribute collection and now combines his passion for history, theatre and opera designing costumes for performances around the globe.
www.christian-lacroix.com/en

Clements Ribeiro are husband and wife duo Suzanne Clements and Inacio Ribeiro, who met at London's Central St Martins and graduated in 1991. Over two decades they have produced eclectic and colourful designs – think Portobello meets Rio, Brazil – and turned cashmere into a striped style staple. Winners of the New Generation Designer of the Year in 1996, Clements Ribeiro went on to be design directors at Cacharel from 2000 until 2007, when they returned to London to re-launch their own label and 'up-cycle' some of their greatest hits.
www.clementsribeiro.com

Diane von Furstenberg is the all-empowering and legendary Belgian-born American fashion designer who created the iconic wrap dress in 1974. From Princess (von Furstenberg) to President (of the CFDA), Diane has been immortalised on the cover of *TIME* and in an Andy Warhol screen-print and her fashion brand is internationally renowned. For her prints, philanthropy, publishing, perfume and pop culture, Diane is the First Lady of Fashion.
www.dvf.com

Fabergé is the Russian jewellery house founded in 1842 in St Petersburg, Imperial Russia, known for dazzling craftsmanship and their most famous commission, the Imperial Easter Eggs. Crafted from gold, jewels, precious metals and stones, each egg was more elaborate than the last. Of the 54 legendary eggs that were made, only 42 have survived and these are prized collectors' items. The house launched fine jewellery in 2009 and is re-establishing the Fabergé name as a leading artisan in gem craftsmanship and fine jewellery innovation. www.faberge.com

Fred Butler creates fun, fashion and above all wearable sculpture. Butler spins together a psychedelic explosion of fashion, music, accessories and art, with her pieces known for adding an unexpected extra dimension to an outfit. Creating showpieces, props and jewellery, she has worked with, among others, Lady Gaga, MTV, Showstudio, Topshop and Swatch. www.fredbutlerstyle.com

Harrods is the iconic Knightsbridge department store, founded in 1824, opening its Brompton Road building in 1849. Harrods showcased the first moving staircase (escalator) in 1898, with smelling salts handed out either end, and has a reputation for selling luxury – whether it's grand pianos, lions or designer labels. The Harrods Bear is a well-loved Christmas tradition and the outfit, designed exclusively by Olivier Rousteing at Balmain, is a scaled down version of one created for Rihanna. www.harrods.com

Henry Holland is the creative *tour-de-force* behind fashion label House of Holland. Mixing irony and a snappy slogan, he first launched his Fashion Groupie T-shirts in 2006 and followed this success six months later with his first show entitled 'One Trick Pony'. He has proved to be anything but and is a hot favourite on the Fashion Week show schedule; he DJs and tweets, and is stocked internationally in high-end boutiques as well as collaborating with the high street. www.houseofholland.co.uk

Hermès is the ultimate luxury label and a timeless status symbol. Originally founded in 1837 as a leather equine and saddle-maker, it's their Kelly and Birkin bags, named after actresses Grace Kelly and Jane Birkin, that remain two of the most coveted handbag designs in the world. Each Kelly bag takes skilled craftsmen twenty hours to make and has a waiting list of around two years. Hermès' iconic printed silk scarves, craftsmanship, leather and logo are unmistakeable global style statements. uk.hermes.com

Holly Fulton studied at Edinburgh College of Art and The Royal College of Art. In 2009 she launched her label, won the Swarovski Emerging Talent Award for Accessories at the British Fashion Awards and was shortlisted for the Vogue Fashion Fund 2015. Referencing Art Deco and Pop Art, Fulton combines digital print and intricate hand-drawing to create a quirky, contemporary and geometric, crystal and Perspex-encrusted take on fashion. www.hollyfulton.com

Jasper Conran is the quintessential English fashion designer and in 2012 was appointed Chairman of The Conran Store. Trained at Parsons School of Design in New York, he launched his first womenswear collection in 1978 and continues to show at London Fashion Week. He has also won acclaim as a costume designer, interior designer and author and is the ultimate connoisseur of good taste, elegance and style and a pioneer in design concept in both fashion and home. www.jasperconran.com

Jean Paul Gaultier created his first piece of haute couture for his teddy bear, Nana. He later designed the conical bra and costumes for Madonna's 1985 Blonde Ambition Tour, founded his own haute couture house in 1997, presented the cult 80s TV series *Eurotrash* and was the creative director at Hermès (2003 – 2010). His bestselling perfume comes in a glass bottle shaped like a torso, he closed his ready-to-wear line in

2014 to focus solely on haute couture, and a retrospective exhibition of his career is currently enjoying a popular world tour.
www.jeanpaulgaultier.com/en

Jo Loves is the new fragrance line created by Jo Malone. She began her career as a facial therapist and soon started to create fragrances and scents for her own products at home, which led her to launch her first brand, Jo Malone. She sold this business to Estée Lauder in 1999, where she remained creative director until 2006. In 2013, after much anticipation, she opened Jo Loves, creating innovative fragrance tapas, scents and new cult memories.
www.joloves.com

Julie Verhoeven is the whimsical British artist and illustrator who has worked across fashion, fine art and illustration. Her work has featured on handbags and high fashion, from Gibo, Cacharel and Louis Vuitton to Mulberry and Versace; and on books and album covers. Verhoeven started work as design assistant at John Galliano then at Martine Sitbon. She is now design academic at both Central St Martins and the Royal College of Art and has had her work exhibited extensively at the Hayward Gallery, The Victoria and Albert Museum and the Institute of Contemporary Art.
www.julieverhoeven.com

Julien Macdonald is all about glamour. The moment he graduated in fashion knitwear from the Royal College, Karl Lagerfeld hired him to design pieces for Chanel haute couture. Two years later, in 1998, encouraged by Isabella Blow, he launched his own label, Mermaids, and has since become a red carpet favourite. He has appeared as a judge on *Britain's Next Top Model*, been creative director at Givenchy and put on his dancing shoes to compete in *Strictly Come Dancing*.
julienmacdonald.com

Liberty's founder 'was determined not to follow fashion but to create new ones'. Arthur Liberty's pioneering spirit led him to travel the world looking for individual pieces to inspire his clientele, and his mock-Tudor London emporium opened in 1875 on Regents Street, stocking ornaments, art fabrics and objets d'art from the East. It continues to showcase the unique and unexpected but always the most beautiful.
www.liberty.co.uk

Lola's Cupcakes began in 2006 when two friends, Victoria Jossel and Romy Lewis, started out with a bake-off and big dreams, and soon had orders flooding in. In 2011 the company was taken over by Asher Budwig, a fourth-generation baker from a family of sweet-toothed entrepreneurs, and the business continues to expand its delicious repertoire of creations.
www.lolas-kitchen.co.uk

Lulu Guinness is the British accessories designer who launched her range of rose basket handbags in 1989 and is now celebrating 25 years in the industry. Guinness creates collectables with a stylish Surrealist twist, and will never be without her trademark red lipstick or Dali-esque lips clutch. Inspired by tomorrow's treasures, pop culture and art, Guinness mixes humour and femininity into her playful signature designs.
www.luluguinness.com

Manolo Blahnik is the most wonderful shoe designer in the world. His story reads like a fable: the Spanish designer founded his label in 1972 after Diana Vreeland told him, 'young man do things, do accessories, do shoes' – and that was it. Inspired by his mother, the arts and moving to London, he has designed shoes for the runway, from Ossie Clark to John Galliano, as well as his own irresistible creations. Much celebrated, his shoes are coveted the world over.
www.manoloblahnik.com

Marian Newman is the Queen of Nails. Her incredible career includes over 50 British *Vogue* covers to date. She has worked with Mario Testino, Patrick Demarchelier, Kate Moss, Lady Gaga, Naomi Campbell, as well as the top nail care companies in the world. Working closely with photographer Nick Knight she created the nails for the Dior and Lancôme campaigns, and in 2014 launched her own nail collection with MAC Cosmetics.
www.mariannewmannails.com

Markus Lupfer adds sequins to a grey day, and wit to knit. Born in Kisslegg, Germany, he graduated from the University of Westminster in 1997 and launched his own label the following season. A London Fashion Week favourite, his cheeky prints, bold knits and humorous embellishments have earned him a devoted A-list following and clientele.
markuslupfer.com

Mary McCartney is an English photographer who specialises in portraits and reportage photography, shooting the unguarded moments that reveal the truth behind her subject. Her work has been featured in numerous galleries and magazines, including the National Portrait Gallery, and collected together in several photography books. She is also the author of *Food* and *At My Table: Vegetarian Food for Family and Friends*.
www.marymccartney.com/ee

Matthew Williamson's debut collection, 'Electric Angels' featured hot pink and icy turquoise pieces and he has continued to wow with a fantastic kaleidoscope of colour, print and bohemian embellishments that ensure the sun always shines on his designs. He has shown at both New York and London Fashion Weeks, and specialises in creating flattering, feminine laid back boho-glamour.
www.matthewwilliamson.com

Michael Howells is fashion's favourite and most original set designer. A modern-day Cecil Beaton with an encyclopaedic imagination, he is both production designer and art director. He works prolifically in film, television, fashion, ballet and theatre, from Douglas McGrath's *Emma* and Sally Potter's *Orlando* to the Rambert Ballet, working with Mario Testino and editorial in *Vogue* as well as creating the most spectacular fashion shows, exhibitions and parties ever imagined. He is also creative director of the Port Eliot Literary Festival.
www.michaelhowellsstudio.com

Nicholas Kirkwood is the much-acclaimed British luxury footwear designer. Graduating from Central St Martins and Cordwainers, he founded his own label in 2004 – and has already won the British Accessories Designer of the Year award three times. His designs challenge footwear and fashion conventions with unique innovative architectural statements. As well as designing for his own collections he has worked alongside Fendi, Erdem, Roksanda Ilincic and Peter Pilotto; was the creative director for Pollini; and mentored the launch of his protégé shoe designer, Sophia Webster.
www.nicholaskirkwood.com

Nick Knight is the pioneering and passionate British fashion photographer, documentary producer, web publisher and director of SHOWstudio, the award-winning fashion website he launched in 2000. From being the first to live-stream and make fashion shows interactive – with McQueen's 'Atlantis' show in 2010 – he has collaborated with everyone in editorial and advertising from John Galliano to Lady Gaga. His work has been published and exhibited globally in fashion, fine art and in his recent solo exhibition, Flora.
showstudio.com

Paul Smith is the British fashion designer whose label is synonymous with British heritage, humour and tailoring. Born in Nottingham, Smith had ambitions to become a professional racing cyclist but had to abandon this dream after a serious accident. While recuperating, he met some art students and started to manage his first boutique before opening his own shop in 1970. He presented his debut menswear label in 1976, and now produces over 14 collections each year. Smith was knighted for his services to fashion in 2000 and is stocked in over 66 countries worldwide.
www.paulsmith.co.uk

Peter Pilotto are the London-based design duo who met in 2000 while studying at Antwerp's Royal Academy of Fine Arts. Peter Pilotto and Christopher De Vos create intricate elegant new classics specialising in bold print, textures and soft sculptural shapes and colourful drapes. They won the BFC/Vogue Designer Fashion Fund of 2014, launched a capsule collection for Target in the same year, and continue to grow in popularity on and off the runway.
www.peterpilotto.com

Piers Atkinson believes he has worn nearly as many hats as he's made – he's an artist, illustrator, milliner, costume designer, party organiser, fashion editor and sometime DJ. After studying graphic design and photography at Bristol University, he worked at Zandra Rhodes before launching his first collection of hats in 2008. Inspired by everything and anything, he has collaborated with designers, celebrities, and on exhibitions, and his hats of humour are available across the globe.
www.piersatkinson.com

Prêt-à-Portea was created by The Berkeley Hotel, London, to add a fashion twist to afternoon tea. With cakes and pastries inspired by the latest catwalk designs, and with a new 'collection' launching every six months, head pastry chef Mourad Khiat mixes sugar and style in this unique afternoon tea. Since launching in 2004, Moschino, Matthew Williamson, Jimmy Choo and McQueen's 'Savage Beauty' have all been baked as biscuits and served with tea in the best British tradition.
www.the-berkeley.co.uk/fashion-afternoon-tea

Rifat Özbek is the Turkish-born fashion and interior designer based in London. He established his own exotic fashion label in 1984, and went on to be named British Designer of the Year in both 1988 and 1992. In 2010 he launched his new business 'Yastik' (Turkish for 'cushion'), mixing his love of colour, fabric and ethnic prints. He now consults as an interior designer for special events.
www.yastikbyrifatozbek.com

Roksanda Ilincic creates striking fashion designs using bold colour with clean architectural cut and graphic lines. Born in Belgrade, Serbia, Ilincic trained to be an architect before moving to London to graduate with an MA in fashion from Central St Martins. She first showed at London Fashion Week in 2003, and opened her first stand-alone store on Mount Street in 2014.
roksanda.com

Roland Mouret is the London-based French fashion master of structure and silhouette. His iconic dresses – including the Galaxy – are instantly recognisable and, such is their status, are known on first-name terms. Born in Lourdes, he worked as a stylist, model and art director before launching his first collection in 1994, as People Corporation, starting a label under his own name in 1998. In 2006 he went into partnership with Simon Fuller and the house and signature continues to grow.
www.rolandmouret.com

Sam McKnight is a big tease. He is one of the most well-respected and accomplished hair stylists of his generation. From editorial to advertising, supermodels to fashion shows, he has long-standing creative collaborations with some of the biggest names in the business, including Nick Knight, Karl Lagerfeld, Mario Testino and Patrick Demarchelier. Whether styling Kate Moss or Princess Diana, Sam has created some of the most iconic images in modern history. He is also a keen baker, gardener and prolific Instagrammer.
www.sammcknight.com

Sara Berman studied fashion at Central St Martins and in 1999, soon after graduation, launched her own label. In 2006 she became creative director for cashmere brand N. Peal. In 2012 Berman decided to swap the fashion world for fine art, and moved away from her own brand to focus on her painting. She lives and paints in London and has been exhibited in several galleries to much acclaim.
www.sarabermanartist.com

Stephen Jones is Britain's leading milliner. Based in London he has created some of the most iconic pieces seen on the catwalks, including those for John Galliano, Marc Jacobs, Vivienne Westwood and Rei Kawakubo. At St Martins he discovered millinery and was a regular at legendary nightclub Blitz, where he met many of his first clients, including Jean Paul Gaultier. In 1980 he opened his salon and in 2009 he co-curated 'Hats: An Anthology' at the V&A. He continues to collaborate in fashion, music and film and is essential at Ascot.
www.stephenjonesmillinery.com

Suzannah has worked in the fashion industry for twenty years as a designer, stylist and trend forecaster. With a nostalgic love of fashion, Suzannah launched her own bespoke label to create unique, feminine designs that create fresh silhouettes with a focus on fabric, finish and flattering cut. From ready-to-wear to couture and bridal appointments, this label ensures well-cut luxury for the well-dressed lady.
www.suzannah.com

Tatty Devine is the fun, independent British jewellery company founded by friends Harriet Vine and Rosie Wolfenden, who met studying fine art at Chelsea School of Art. Designing and hand-making jewellery since 1999, their pieces are colourful and confident. Using Perspex, acrylics, leather, plastics and non-precious fabrics, they are inspired by art, music, fashion, all that's around and having fun.
www.tattydevine.com

Thakoon was the fashion coordinator at *Harpers Bazaar* US by day while studying to become a fashion designer at Parsons School of Art and Design at night. Born in Thailand and raised in Nebraska, he graduated from Boston University and worked in retail and editorial before launching his own label in 2004. With a light, delicate cut and a love of bold print and modern silhouettes, Thakoon had a starring role as a designer to watch in R.J. Cutler's 2009 cult documentary about *American Vogue*, *The September Issue*.
www.thakoon.com

Theodora & Callum is the latest collaboration between acclaimed fashion luminary Stefani Greenfield and entertainment producer Desiree Gruber. Born out of a love for collecting beautiful things from all over the world, Theodora & Callum is an accessories-based line featuring scarves, jewellery, dresses, tops, trousers and caftans inspired by their travels. Named after Greenfield's daughter and Gruber's son, Theodora & Callum is a highly personal brand – it's not about chasing trends, it's about sharing and wearing what you love.
www.theodoraandcallum.com

Topshop is the home of fast, fun, affordable fashion, its flagship at the heart of Oxford Circus, London. Founded in 1964 as an offshoot to Peter Robinson, it is now the jewel in the Arcadia Group crown with over 400 stores in around 40 countries. Topshop launched Kate Moss's own collection, sponsors young fashion designers, presents its own 'Unique' collection as part of London Fashion Week, and is every fashion girl's essential label. www.topshop.com

Val Garland is one of fashion's leading and innovative make-up artists. Imaginative, colourful and creative, she has been responsible for numerous magazine covers and fashion shows. Working on shows for Alexander McQueen, Mary Katrantzou, Nick Knight and Mario Testino, among others, Garland is a chameleon, creating a new face for every occasion. From her iconic eyes to sugar lips, make-up for Lady Gaga or Kate Moss, this MAC ambassador makes the world look beautiful. instagram.com/thevalgarland

Vicki Sarge is the London-based jewellery designer who creates bold statements by infusing hand-crafted jewellery with her rock'n'roll spirit. The Detroit-born designer was co-founder and designer of Erickson Beamon before she launched her own brand in 2014. Sarge has collaborated with designers including Dries van Noten and John Galliano and also launched Sam McKnight's debut hair accessories range, 'Floramorta'. www.vickisarge.com

Wild at Heart was founded in 1993 by Nikki Tibbles. Famous for their opulent style, each bouquet is handmade with love and inspired by art and fashion as much as the English countryside and seasonal blooms. Nikki and her team have decorated weddings, events, shows and homes; from single arrangements to architectural displays – using nature to transform any space into something beautiful. www.wildatheart.com

ACKNOWLEDGEMENTS

This book is beautiful because of the people who are part of it, and because of everyone who believed in yet another of my crazy ideas. Thank you to all the designers who indulged me, for all these projects, your time and more, and for still taking my calls at the end of it. Thank you to my agent Simon Trewin for being rock'n'roll, my editor Jocasta Hamilton for bringing beauty to life, and to my amazing family and friends, especially Hugh Devlin for being a voice of calm, Natalie Theo for the help and hot chocolates, Tess Richards for making the sewing make sense, Alex Fury, Ben Seidler, Andrew Lamb, Nicholas Kirkwood and Narmin Mohammadi, and all those who had faith in me – and this book – even when I didn't.

PICTURE CREDITS

Endpages artwork created by Ben Seidler

PHOTOGRAPHY
Nick Knight: p. 110, p. 113, p. 114, p. 115
Andrew Lamb: p. 30, p. 31, p. 34, p. 35, p. 36, p. 56, p. 94, p. 96, p. 97, p. 134, p. 135, p. 146, p. 149
Mary McCartney: p. 130, p. 132, p. 133
Jacob Perlmutter: p. 2/121, p. 6, p. 9, p. 10, p. 12, p. 13, p. 24, p. 27, p. 28, p. 48, p. 49, p. 51, p. 58, p. 59, p. 74, p. 75, p. 76, p. 100, p. 118, p. 119, p. 121, p. 126, p. 129, p. 154, p. 200, p. 202

PORTRAITS
Anya Hindmarch p. 163 by Andrew Woofinden
Bella Freud p. 29 by Mary McCartney
Charlotte Olympia p. 52 by Alexandra Leese
Fred Butler p. 71 by Jenny Lewis
Lulu Guinness p. 170 by Stefan Sieler
Manolo Blahnik p. 117 by Michael Roberts
Mary McCartney p. 131 by Tracy Gilbert
Markus Lupfer p. 66 by Andrew Vowles
Matthew Williamson p. 15 by Miguel Domingos
Paul Smith p. 18 by James Mooney
Tatty Devine p. 139 by Holly Falconer
Sara Berman p. 147 by David Scheinmann
Stephen Jones p. 44 by Hyea Won Kang

The Hermès Project, pp. 134–137, is reproduced with thanks and the kind permission of Hermès, AM-PM and Alice Charbin. Model concept and realisation by Muriel Abecassis & Philippe Moyen (Agence AM-PM). Illustrations by Alice Charbin.

HERMES Kelly © bag. The name and shape of the Kelly bag are the full and entire property of Hermès. The use of the model provided does not give the user any intellectual property rights.

All other images, illustrations and concepts are the intellectual property of the respective designers.

"SHE REFUSED TO BE BORED CHIEFLY BECAUSE...